First World War
and Army of Occupation
War Diary
France, Belgium and Germany

42 DIVISION
125 Infantry Brigade
Lancashire Fusiliers
1/6th Battalion
1 March 1917 - 11 January 1918

WO95/2654/3

The Naval & Military Press Ltd
www.nmarchive.com
Published in association with The National Archives

Published by

The Naval & Military Press Ltd

Unit 10 Ridgewood Industrial Park,
Uckfield, East Sussex,
TN22 5QE England
Tel: +44 (0) 1825 749494

www.naval-military-press.com

www.nmarchive.com

This diary has been reprinted in facsimile from the original. Any imperfections are inevitably reproduced and the quality may fall short of modern type and cartographic standards.

© **Crown Copyright**
Images reproduced by permission of The National Archives, London, England, 2015.

Contents

Document type	Place/Title	Date From	Date To
Heading	WO95/2654/3 125 Infantry Brigade 1/6 Battalion Lancashire Fusiliers Mar 1917-Jan 1918		
Heading	42nd Division 125th Infy Bde 1-6th, Bn. Lancs Fus. Mar 1917-1918 Jan To 66 Div 198 Bde Vol 2. Vol 12 Blue No Vol 20-Vol 30		
Heading	War Diary Of 1/6th Bttn The Lancashire Fusiliers From 1.9.17 To 31.3.17 Volume 20. Mar 17 Jan 18		
War Diary	Pont Remy Ref Map Abbeville 14	01/03/1917	01/03/1917
War Diary	Sorel Wanel	02/03/1917	02/03/1917
War Diary	Ref Map Abbeville 14 France 1-100000	03/03/1917	11/03/1917
War Diary	Sorel Wanel Maps France 1:100.000 Abbille 14 Dieppe 16	12/03/1917	14/03/1917
War Diary	Hamel Ref Map France 62q 1:40.000 Amiens. 17 1:100000	15/03/1917	18/03/1917
War Diary	Hamel Map. France Amiens 17. 1:100,000 France 62d 1:40000	19/03/1917	24/03/1917
War Diary	Eclusier	25/03/1917	31/03/1917
Heading	War Diary Of 1/6th Bttn The Lancashire Fusiliers From 1.4.17 To 30.4.17 Vol No. 21		
War Diary	Eclusier Map Ref France 1:100000 Amiens. 17 62d Ed 1:40,000	01/04/1917	04/04/1917
War Diary	Peronne	05/04/1917	08/04/1917
War Diary	Longavesnes 62c E. 25	09/04/1917	09/04/1917
War Diary	Saulgourt 62c E.9.d.	10/04/1917	13/04/1917
War Diary	Villers Faucon 28b. 2.9	14/04/1917	14/04/1917
War Diary	Peronne	15/04/1917	16/04/1917
War Diary	Eclusier	17/04/1917	21/04/1917
War Diary	Peronne 62c. 1.2 D.O.10	22/04/1917	28/04/1917
War Diary	Buire	29/04/1917	30/04/1917
War Diary	War Diary Of 1/6th Bttn The Lancashire Fusiliers. From 1.5.17 To 31.5.17 Vol. No. 22		
Heading	War Diary May 1917 1/6th Bn The Lancashire Fusiliers Vol 22		
War Diary	Villers Faucon Map Ref 62c E. 29. c. 1.9	01/05/1917	01/05/1917
War Diary	Lempire F. 16.a.9.6	02/05/1917	04/05/1917
War Diary	Villers Faucon E22. D. 55	05/05/1917	07/05/1917
War Diary	Villers Faucon E. 22.d. 55 Epehy F.1d. 64	08/05/1917	12/05/1917
War Diary	Battn. HQ No. 13 Copsc F. 3.C 9.9	13/05/1917	16/05/1917
War Diary	No 13 Copse F 3.c 99	17/05/1917	18/05/1917
War Diary	Villers Faucon F 22a 9.4	19/05/1917	19/05/1917
War Diary	Equancourt V 10.a. 1.6 57.c	20/05/1917	21/05/1917
War Diary	Goozeaucourt Wood 27 Q 22c 3.3	22/05/1917	25/05/1917
War Diary	In The Line Ref Map 57c. 5E. R 13a 1.7	26/05/1917	27/05/1917
War Diary	Ytres. Ref Map. 57c P. 20d.	28/05/1917	31/05/1917
Miscellaneous	O.C. C. Coy B 125 App I	27/05/1917	27/05/1917
Heading	War Diary of 1/6th. Battalion The Lancashire Fusiliers. From:- 1st June, 1917. To:- 30th, June, 1917 (Volume 23).		
War Diary	Ytres P	01/06/1917	04/06/1917
War Diary	Havrincourt Wood Q	05/06/1917	12/06/1917

War Diary	Q 7b.3.4	13/06/1917	16/06/1917
War Diary	Havrincourt Wood Q	17/06/1917	21/06/1917
War Diary	Ytres P	22/06/1917	30/06/1917
Heading	War Diary Of 1/6 Batt. Lancs. Fus. For. 1st July 1917 31st July/1917 Vol 24		
War Diary	Ytres 57 c Se P 20 d.	01/07/1917	05/07/1917
War Diary	Gomiecourt 57c A 22d	06/07/1917	31/07/1917
Heading	War Diary Of 1/6th Battn Lancashire Fusiliers Vol No 25 1 August 1917-31/8/1917 Vol 7		
War Diary	Gomiecourt 57 C A 29 d	01/08/1917	20/08/1917
War Diary	Bouzincourt	21/08/1917	22/08/1917
War Diary	Sheet 27 L 8 C 73	22/08/1917	29/08/1917
War Diary	Sheet 28 N.W. H 18 1-7095	30/08/1917	30/08/1917
War Diary	Frezenburg 1/10000 C 30 b 29	31/08/1917	31/08/1917
Heading	War Diary Of 1/6th Bn. The Lancashire Fusiliers From 1.9.17-30/9/17 Volume No. 26		
War Diary	Frezenburg 1/10,000 C 36P 89	01/09/1917	01/09/1917
War Diary	Sheet 28 N.W. 1/10,000 I 5a 28	02/09/1917	06/09/1917
War Diary	Sheet 28 Gile 72	08/09/1917	14/09/1917
War Diary	Sheet 28 N.W. 1/10000 I 5.a 2.8	15/09/1917	17/09/1917
War Diary	Sheet 28 G 11.c 7.2	18/09/1917	18/09/1917
War Diary	Sheet 27 N.E L. 3. B Central	19/09/1917	22/09/1917
War Diary	Hazebrouck 5A	23/09/1917	24/09/1917
War Diary	Sheet 19 D 22	25/09/1917	25/09/1917
War Diary	Sheet 11 S.E. WII C. Central	26/09/1917	30/09/1917
Heading	War Diary of 1/6th Battalion The Lancashire Fusiliers. From 1.10.17 To 31.10.17 Volume No. 27		
War Diary	Sheet 11 SE W II C Centreal	01/10/1917	05/10/1917
War Diary	Sheet 5 M 28 Central	06/10/1917	18/10/1917
War Diary	Reuport Sector Sh5 M28 C Vd & M21 d m 27b	19/10/1917	20/10/1917
War Diary	Sh 11 SE X B b	21/10/1917	21/10/1917
War Diary	Sh 11SE N 15a	22/10/1917	29/10/1917
War Diary	Sh11SE X 13.b	30/10/1917	31/10/1917
Operation(al) Order(s)	Battalion Order No. 125	19/10/1917	19/10/1917
Operation(al) Order(s)	1/6th Lancashire Fusiliers. Battalion Operation Order No. 123	12/10/1917	12/10/1917
Operation(al) Order(s)	Battalion Operation Order No. 127	26/10/1917	26/10/1917
Operation(al) Order(s)	1/6th Lancashire Fusiliers. Battalion Operation Order No. 128	02/10/1917	02/10/1917
Operation(al) Order(s)	1/6th Lancashire Fusiliers. Battalion Operation Order No. 124	16/10/1917	16/10/1917
Operation(al) Order(s)	Battalion Operation Order No. 129	20/10/1917	20/10/1917
Heading	1/6th Lancashire Fusiliers War Diary Vol. 28 November 1917 1/11/1917-30/11/1917		
War Diary	Ph 11SE. X 13b	01/11/1917	06/11/1917
War Diary	SH 5. In22. In28	07/11/1917	10/11/1917
War Diary	Place Sh 5 M 28	11/11/1917	18/11/1917
War Diary	Cost-Dunkerque Shla 15a 1/100000 Sh 11 & 19 1/40,000	19/11/1917	19/11/1917
War Diary	Shts 19 & 27 1/400000	20/11/1917	20/11/1917
War Diary	Sh 27 1/40000	21/11/1917	22/11/1917
War Diary	Place. 1/20000 Sh. 27. 36a 1/40000	23/11/1917	23/11/1917
War Diary	Thiennes (map 36a I 22a)	24/11/1917	27/11/1917
War Diary	Oblinghem (map 36a W. 29)	28/11/1917	28/11/1917
War Diary	Givenchy (map 36c A 8c)	29/11/1917	30/11/1917

Heading	War Diary of 1/6th Battalion The Lancashire Fusiliers. From 1.12.17 To 31.12.17 Volume No. 29. App 1, 2, 3, 4, 5, 6, 7, 8		
War Diary	Givenchy (map 36c A. 8.c)	01/12/1917	03/12/1917
War Diary	Cuinchy (map 36c A. 15)	04/12/1917	10/12/1917
War Diary	Bethune 1.40000. E 17 b9.9	11/12/1917	21/12/1917
War Diary	Bethune 1,40,000	22/12/1917	22/12/1917
War Diary	Gorre F3 b 55	23/12/1917	27/12/1917
War Diary	Gorre F3 G-55 also 36c N.W.1. & 36, S.W.3 La Bassee v Richzbouig	28/12/1917	31/12/1917
Operation(al) Order(s)	1/6th Lancashire Fusiliers. Battalion Operation Order No. 141	03/12/1917	03/12/1917
Miscellaneous	War Diary		
Operation(al) Order(s)	1/6th Lancashire Fusiliers Battalion Operation Order No. 142	08/12/1917	08/12/1917
Operation(al) Order(s)	1/6th Lancashire Fusiliers Battalion Operation Order No. 143 App 3	08/12/1917	08/12/1917
Operation(al) Order(s)	1/6th Battalion The Lancashire Fusiliers. Correction To Battalion Operation Order No. 143. App. 4	09/12/1917	09/12/1917
Operation(al) Order(s)	1/6th Lancashire Fusiliers. Battalion Operation Order No. 143 App. 5	08/12/1917	08/12/1917
Operation(al) Order(s)	1/6th Bn. Lancashire Fusiliers. Battalion Operation Order No. 145 App. 6	21/12/1917	21/12/1917
Operation(al) Order(s)	1/6th Battalion The Lancashire Fusiliers. Battalion Warning Order No. 146 App 4	26/12/1917	26/12/1917
Operation(al) Order(s)	1/6th Battalion Lancashire Fusiliers. Battalion Operation Order No. 147 App. 8	27/12/1917	27/12/1917
Miscellaneous	Office Scheme	29/12/1917	29/12/1917
Heading	War Diary of 1/6th Battalion The Lancashire Fusiliers From 1.1.18 To 31.1.18 Volume No. 30 App 1, 2, 3, 4, 5, 6, 7, 8, 9, 10		
War Diary	La Bassee 36c NW Richebourg 36 S.W Cs 26 b. 5.0)	01/01/1918	03/01/1918
War Diary	La Bassee 36c N.W.A 8c 82	04/01/1918	08/01/1918
War Diary	La Bassee 36c N.W. Richeburg. 36 S.W. (S26b 50)	09/01/1918	11/01/1918
War Diary	La Bassee 36c N.W. Richebourg 36 S.W. (S26b50)	12/01/1918	16/01/1918
War Diary	Beuvry 36 B N.E. 2. 1/10.000 E. 6 C.	17/01/1918	23/01/1918
War Diary	Beuvry 36B. N.E. 2 1/10.000 E 6C	24/01/1918	28/01/1918
War Diary	Beuvry 36B. N.E. 2 1/10,000 E 6C. F 1Dc.	29/01/1918	31/01/1918
Operation(al) Order(s)	1/6th Battalion The Lancashire Fusiliers. Battalion Warning Order No. 148	01/01/1918	01/01/1918
Operation(al) Order(s)	1/6th Battalion The Lancashire Fusiliers. Battalion Operation Order No. 149	02/01/1918	02/01/1918
Operation(al) Order(s)	Defence Scheme Support Battalion App 3	07/01/1918	07/01/1918
Miscellaneous	2/L Sutherland		
Operation(al) Order(s)	1/6th Battalion The Lancashire Fusiliers. Battalion Operation Order No. 150 App 4		
War Diary	Defence Scheme App. 5	11/01/1918	11/01/1918
Operation(al) Order(s)	1/6th Battalion The Lancashire Fusiliers, Battalion Operation Order No. 151 App 6	13/01/1918	13/01/1918
Operation(al) Order(s)	Corrigendum To Battalion Operation Order No. 151 App. 7	14/01/1918	14/01/1918
Miscellaneous	1/6th Battalion The Lancashire Fusiliers. Addendum No. 1. to Battalion Operation Order No. 151 App. 8	16/01/1918	16/01/1918
Miscellaneous	C.C.A. Company App. 9	19/01/1918	19/01/1918
Operation(al) Order(s)	1/6th Battalion The Lancashire Fusiliers Battalion Operation Order No. 152. App 10	27/01/1918	27/01/1918

Miscellaneous   2/Lt Sutherland

③ WO95/2654

125 Infantry Brigade

1/6 Battalion Lancashire Fusiliers

Mar 1917 – Jan 1918

42ND DIVISION
125TH INFY BDE

1-6TH. BN LANCS FUS.
MAR 1917-~~MAR 1919~~.
1918 JAN

TO 66 DIV 198 BDE

VOL 2 — VOL 12   BLUE NO
VOL 20 — VOL 30

Vol 2.

19.J.
Oakes

Oakes

CONFIDENTIAL.
WAR DIARY.
OF.
1/6ᵗʰ BTTN THE LANCASHIRE FUSILIERS.

FROM 1.3.17   TO 31.3.17.

VOLUME 20.

Mar '17
Jan '18

Army Form C. 2118.

WAR DIARY
or
INTELLIGENCE SUMMARY.
(Erase heading not required)

VOL. 20.

1/6th Lancashire Fusiliers

Place	Date 1917	Hour	Summary of Events and Information	Strength O	Strength OR		Remarks and references to Appendices
PONT REMY Rd. Map ABBEVILLE 1/4	MARCH 1.	nil	Btn. arrived at PONT REMY at 2030. detrained and marched to SOREL and WANEL. Btn. HQ and 2 companies billeted in SOREL and 2 companies in WANEL.			Wet & very cold.	A.A.
SOREL + WANEL	2.	nil	Arrived at SOREL at 0300 and WANEL at 0340. all clear	21	896	cold.	A.A.B.
Ref. map ABBEVILLE 1/4 FRANCE N 20,000	3.	nil	Route march by companies. all clear	21	896	cold.	A.A.B.
"	4.	nil	Church Parade. — all clear	21	896	Snow. 2"	A.A.B.
"	5.	nil	Complete transport on Pair E.T. scale drawn from ABBEVILLE. all clear	21	896	cold.	A.A.B.
"	6.	nil	Rifles ment. VII drawn complete with bayonets etc. all clear	21	896	Hard frost	A.A.B.
"	7.	nil	Company training, bayonet fighting physical drill. all clear	21	897	Snow, hard frost	A.A.B.
"	8.	nil	Training either for Bombing, Bayonet fighting, a drill allowed by G.S.O. 42 Div. all clear	21	897	Snow, hard frost	A.A.B.
"	9.	nil	Btn. Route march 2½ hours. Route followed SOREL-FONTAINE-PONT-REMY-SIN + RETURN.	21	898	Snow	A.A.B.
"	10.	nil	Shooting drive for NCOs all clear	22	878	Thaws & rain	A.A.B.
"	11.	Instructions from 126 Bde. to hold Btn in readiness to move at short notice. Sunday without casualties all clear		22	871		A.A.B.

WAR DIARY
INTELLIGENCE SUMMARY
(Erase heading not required.)

Instructions regarding War Diaries and Intelligence Summaries are contained in F.S. Regs., Part II and the Staff Manual respectively. Title pages will be prepared in manuscript.

Army Form C. 2118.

Place	Date 1917	Hour	Summary of Events and Information				Remarks and references to Appendices
SOREL HAMEL Maps FRANCE 1:100,000 ABVILLE 14 DIEPPE 16.	Mar 12		Maps FRANCE 1:100,000 ABVILLE 14 Issued from DIEPPE 16. (& Bde HQ). Orders recd to send 200 men to Course at PONT REMY School of Musketry on 14th inst.	all clear	8 8rough	O. O2.	M.R.
	13		Orders from 101 Bde to send on all transport to HAMEL starting on the 15th for lines transport and billeting parties only.		22	S65 cold	
			Company training as before	all clear	22	862 frost	
"	14		Adv'nt for move of Bttn (- 1st Bde (group) recd from 101 Bde dld 14.3.17 (to be sent by Fwd Chain to 101 Bde detach Corbie march to Hamel) 1st line transport despatches to HAMEL today starting 8 AM. Billeting Officer, interpreters and 1st Bde Adv'nt party to average 3 billets for transport and Btn on arrival at HAMEL detrain on 19th inst	all clear	22	861 Warmer rain	M.R. O.5 Bde Orders No 2.
HAMEL Ref Map France 62c 1:40,000	15		3 large trains were of 101 Corps front Rail 1:20,000. Concerted to 3.3.17.	Btn entrained at LONGRÉ leaving train from SOREL, HAMEL there road heads from WAHEL. Battalion (305) pushed to CORBIE via AMIENS detrained at CORBIE 1500 and handed to HAMEL Btn accommodated in 8 large huts capable of holding 100 men.	19	651 Cold	M.R.
AMIENS:17 1:100,000	16			Coy training for 3 hours burning rubbish	19	561	2.2
"	17			Coy training for 5 hours	29	689	-
"	18		Instructions recd from 101 Bde to act up authorisation of officers in exc to instruction in the lines every other day for 40 hours.	Co lectured & coy rec went to view time fray fortifications instruction	all clear	25	680	M.R.

1577 Wt W10791/1773 500,000 1/15 D.D. & L. A.D.S.S./Forms/C. 2118.

Army Form C. 2118.

WAR DIARY
or
INTELLIGENCE SUMMARY.
(Erase heading not required.)

Instructions regarding War Diaries and Intelligence Summaries are contained in F.S. Regs., Part II. and the Staff Manual respectively. Title pages will be prepared in manuscript.

Place	Date 1917	Hour	Summary of Events and Information		Strength		Remarks and references to Appendices
HAMEL	MAR.		following maps red from 1/2 Bde		O.	68.	h.R.
Map France 17 AMIENS. M. 1/100,000 FRANCE 63A 1/40,000	19.		FRANCE. AMIENS. 17 62.D 62.C.SE 62.C.SA.S.w 62.C.EA.I N.W. Europe 1908 Pl.	Platoons are now being organised according to the principles laid down in S.S. 144. Normal training for the attack.	all clear	25.	678	Cold	h.R.
"	20.		—nil—	1 officer & (C.S.M. sent up to the line for 48 hours instruction. Scheme of training all ranks in the use and operation of their own particular branch continued. The lecture by div.co-ordnr on Battle front. Throwing of all ranks in gas.	all clear	26.	656	Cold	h.R.
"	21.		—nil—	Training of all ranks in gas and bomb throwing. Skirmisher training in Lewis Gun Rifle Grenades, Bayonet, Signalling.	all clear	26.	659	Cold & damp	h.R.
"	22.		BAB Coord received from trenches SS 534.	Whole Btn. took the small box respirator during the day. Specialist training in Lewis Gun, Rifle Grenades Signalling Bombing & gas.	all clear	29.	868	Frost	h.R.
"	23.		—nil—	Coys platoon training in musketry, Lewis gun, Rifle grenade, Signalling, Bombing & gas during morning. Baths (hot) for men in the afternoon.	all clear	29.	866	Frost & Snow	
"	24.		orders recd to send 1 Coy to R. de D. 92 next 62 D. to furnish fatigue for the loading Coal. Orders for move of B.M. to ECLUSIER, PRISE FEUILLERE recd.	Coys & platoon training in musketry Lewis guns. etc. Rifle grenades bombing & gas. Lewis gun firing on ranges. Summer training adopted today 11.am because daylight	all clear	29.	877	fine & dry	IX-Bde order No 3 h.R.

Army Form C. 2118.

WAR DIARY
or
INTELLIGENCE SUMMARY.
(Erase heading not required.)

Instructions regarding War Diaries and Intelligence Summaries are contained in F.S. Regs., Part II. and the Staff Manual respectively. Title pages will be prepared in manuscript.

Place	Date	Hour	Summary of Events and Information	Strength		Remarks and references to Appendices
				O.	O.R.	
ECLUSIER	1917 Mar 25	Map 62C AMIENS 17.	Bn. proceeded by hand route (in Bde.) to ECLUSIER via CERISY, MORCOURT, MÉRICOURT, PROISY, ECLUSIER. Left 7.05 a.m. arrived 3.15 pm. 100 yds distance between platoons. 1st line transport accompanied Bn.	0.	Bn. accommodated in huts and villas.	L.R.
"	26		Total of 400 men & 12 officers to go on working parties tomorrow.	22	650	L.R.
"	27		Instructions received from 145 Bde. for 200 men & 7 officers to proceed to BARLEUX tomorrow for working party. Working parties as follows:- 6 off. 200 men to BARLEUX 6 off. 200 men " HERBÉCOURT Work road mending under Pioneer. Started 7.0 a.m. returned 4.0 pm.	23	648	L.R.
"	28		Instructions rec'd. from 145 Bde. for 400 men to be again working tomorrow. Working party as follows:- 7 off. 400 men to BARLEUX 8 am Returned. Work road mending under pioneers.	23	654	
"	29		Instructions rec'd from 145 Bde. for 300 men to go as working party to FLAUCOURT. Working parties as follows:- 6 off. 200 men to BARLEUX 6 off. 100 men " HERBÉCOURT Work road mending under pioneer. Left 7.0 a.m. returned 4.0 pm.	20	644	hard frost in morning, snow in afternoon
"	30		Instructions rec'd from 145 Bde. for 700 men to work on BARLEUX-HERBÉCOURT Road. Working parties as follows:- 7 off. & 300 men to BARLEUX 7 off. & 300 men " HERBÉCOURT Work road mending with pioneers.	20	633	Heavy frost rain.
"	31		Instructions from 145 Bde for 500 men to be employed working party. Working parties as follows:- 5 off. & 200 men to BARLEUXVIR HERBÉCOURT & BARLEUX work road mending party on BARLEUX road.	23	519	
				20	585	L.R.

R.L.Lees Lt.Colonel
Cmdg 1/6th Lan Fus

1.4.17.

Vol 3

20. J.
6 sheets
Howard

CONFIDENTIAL.
WAR DIARY
OF
1/6th BATTN THE LANCASHIRE FUSILIERS

FROM. 1.4.17   TO   30.4.17.

VOL. No. 21.

Army Form C. 2118.

WAR DIARY
or
INTELLIGENCE SUMMARY.

(Erase heading not required.)

VOL. 21.

1/6 Bth. The Lancashire Fusiliers.

Place	Date	Hour	Summary of Events and Information	Strength	Weather	Remarks and references to Appendices
ECLUSIER. MAP REF. FRANCE/MODO AMIENS. 62.d E.4.7. 1/40,000	April 1917. 1		Instructions recd from 125 Bde to send 200 working party our tunnel	8 OR 582	Cold wet	L. in R.
	2		To officers & 350 men supplied a working party today to work on the HERBECOURT BIACHE Road under Pioneers. Rode from 8:30 am till 4.0 pm. When tools were drawn. Work chiefly consisted of filling holes in the road and digging dirt alongside for draining. It rained all the time.	19. 582	Wet	L. in R.
			To officers and 380 men supplied a working party today. Work was again on the HERBECOURT BIAGNE Road. The same work as heretofore. No limber war taken this day. Hours of work as usual 8.30 am to 4.0 pm.	19. 604	do	R. in R.
"	3		7 Officers & 250 men working party today. HERBECOURT BIACHE road approx 62 c H. 34 a. Hours of work as usual.	19. 531	do	L. in R.
"	4		7 Officers & all available men found working party HERBECOURT BIACHE Road approx 62 c H. 38 d and H. 29 c. Hours of work as usual. Only 270 men available	19 520	do	L. in R.
PERONNE.	5		B[attalio]n moved to PERONNE on instructions from 125 Bde. orders were received on arrival at 62 c H.30.c.99. Working parties were recalled but were ordered to PERONNE instead of ECLUSIER. Now located about 5.0 pm. Bth Billeted in Cellars and ruined houses. Accommodation for Bn Hdrs has to be obtained from River SOMME.	19 520	Fine day	L. in R.
"	6		All available ranks found working party on road 62 e O.6. a. 2. 9. where every line blown up a tank in the Bad work consists of filling in Crater & draining road which is very bad.	19. 500	Cold wet	L. in R.
"	7		All available ranks on working party 62 c O.6. a. 99. Continue work on the road as before.	19. 518	do	L. in R.

1577 Wt. W10791/1773 500,000 1/15 D. D. & L. A.D.S.S./Forms/C. 2118.

WAR DIARY
or
INTELLIGENCE SUMMARY.
(Erase heading not required.)

Army Form C. 2118.

Instructions regarding War Diaries and Intelligence Summaries are contained in F. S. Regs., Part II. and the Staff Manual respectively. Title pages will be prepared in manuscript.

Place	Date 1917 APRIL	Hour	Important orders Rec'd	Summary of Events and Information	Strength	Weather	Remarks and references to Appendices
	8		The Bn. is to move to LONGAVESNES on the 10th inst. and SAULCOURT on the 11th inst. The 175 Bde is to take over a sector of the line now occupied by the 143 Bde.	All available all ranks continue working on the Roads. The group system in use by the 50th Div has been adopted and works exceedingly well. Each group knows who is in charge of them and what they have to do, and any portion of the work is badly done responsibility can be fixed.	18	wet	Bde Order No 4. Apx Q
LONGAVESNES 62C.E.95.	9		Nil.	Bn. moved to LONGAVESNES and bivouaced. Accommodation is bad here as the enemy has destroyed every building in this retreat.	18	wet	Apx R
SAULCOURT 62C.E.9.d.	10		Working party to work on road leading from S of SAULCOURT (62c) to EPEHY.	Bn. moved to SAULCOURT. We are now in support of 7th Army in the left section of the line from MALASSISE FARM (62c.F.8.a.10.0) to EPEHY STATION (62c.1.B.central). The four hours spent quiet but for occasional shelling of the village of SAULCOURT. Seldom more than 6 shells at a time. H.V. guns fired from long range with HE charge. We took over from the 17th R.W. Regt.	17	wet	Apx R
11		Instructions rec'd to move 7th L.F. into the line on 12th inst.	Working Party worked on road from 62c.E.10.c.7.9 to 62c.E.5.c.87.) The road is being bad and has holes 10" deep in surface which have to be filled with grano.	17	wet	Bde Orders No 5. Apx R

WAR DIARY
or
INTELLIGENCE SUMMARY
(Erase heading not required.)

Army Form C. 2118.

VOL. 21.

1/6th Bn. The Lancashire Fusiliers

Place	Date APRIL 1917	Hour	Important Orders Rec'd	Summary of Events and Information	Strength	Weather	Remarks and references to Appendices
SAULCOURT 62°E.9.d	12.		The Relief due for the 12th inst. is postponed till the 13th inst. 2 Coys to be moved up to the 7th L.F. in Roisel sector at dusk.	Work as usual. Carried out on roads. 2 no coys. 1/6 L.F. moved up to the 7th L.F. at Epehy in the Catt sector at F.1.a.55 to be placed in reserve for that Bn.	16	499 Warm & Dry	M.R.
	13.		Programme Med. that the Bn. will be Relieved tonight. We will be relieved Coy by Coy & be Regt & move to PERONNE via VILLERS FAUCON.	The Bn. Relieved the 7th L.F. in the right sector of Bde. front. Relief complete above midnight. Line held in general line from F.1.a.10.10. to F.2. C.3.1. along the railway cutting with posts at MALASSISE FARM. No.12 Copse and TETARD WOOD. Nothing to Report during the night. Whole front fairly quiet.	16	499 Wet	Bn. Order No.7. L.O.R.
VILLERS FAUCON. 28.6.29.	14.		Nil.	The Bn. Relieved at EPEHY by the 7th L.F. in the right sector of Bde. front leaving without much observation. No 12 Coy of MALASSISE Farm were shelled quite considerably. Casualties were 2 K.I.A. and small calibre shrapnel. The Bn. was relieved by the 5th S.W. Regt & arrived at VILLERS FAUCON about 2.0.a.m.	20	628 do	Bn. Order No. J. L.O.R.
PERONNE	15.		3 Working parties required on roads.	The village of EPEHY was shelled during the day fairly heavily but without much observation.	21	664 Fine	
	16.		The Bn. will move to PERONNE via PERONNE FRISE area tomorrow. The Bn. to incur to ECLUSIER.	Bn. marched to PERONNE via DRIENCOURT where the Bn. was billeted in celler etc. Same quartre occupied on left. Working party of 50 men turned out 11.0 pm to unload rails from train but were not required (they returned at 2.0.a.m.	21	664 Cold & Wet	
				3 Working parties detailed, worked on roads as usual from 8.15 am to 4.0 pm.	22	682 Wet	Bde. Order No. 8.
ECLUSIER.	17.		Nil	Bn. marched to ECLUSIER arriving at 5.0 pm in back a debt. Same area taken over.	22	682 Wet	
"	18.		Nil	Training for 3 days (which being been asked by Brigadier & working parties commenced. 80 men as working party to town Major at Cappy. Bn. Baths work and about 200 bathes bathed.	22	682 Wet	

Army Form C. 2118.

WAR DIARY
or
INTELLIGENCE SUMMARY.
(Erase heading not required.)

1/4 Bn. The Lancashire Fusiliers   VOL 21.

Instructions regarding War Diaries and Intelligence Summaries are contained in F.S. Regs., Part II. and the Staff Manual respectively. Title pages will be prepared in manuscript.

Place	Date	Hour	Summary of Events and Information	Remarks and references to Appendices
ECLUSIER	19		Bn. continues reorganisation when on the platoon system. Special training. CS.1143. Preeve arena carried out by corps. Bn. find duty coys. 10 Officer & 440 men provide working party to TOWN MAJOR at CAPPY.	L.u.R
"	20		Bde to move to PERONNE area. Bn. to turn to PERONNE on 22nd. Continuation of reorganisation of Bn. 1 Offr & 40 men provide working party at CAPPY as before.	Bde order No.9 Wan 22,682 day 1
"	21		nil.	Continuation of reorganisation as before.	L.u.R 22,665 -do-
PERONNE 62c.I.27.d.00	22		Bn. moved to PERONNE arriving at noon. Accommodated in cellars & buildings. Accommodation good.	L.u.R 22,656 -
"	23		nil	Map Ref 4 Bn-62c I.27.d 0.10. 3 Coys working on road from PERONNE to DOINGT. 2 Coys working on 60cm Decauville Rail at Blanches.	L.u.R 22,674. -
"	24		nil	2 Coys on Roads and 2 Coys on Railway at BIACHES as before. Bn. Baths have been built and about 200 men can be bathed daily.	L.u.R 22,660 -
"	25		nil	Working parties as usual. All guards are hitherto supplied by the 1/2 Bde are gradually being taken over by this Bde. Chiefly by this Bn. on the remainder of the Bde to Rancourt.	L.u.R 21,564 -
"	26		nil	Working parties as usual.	L.u.R 24,546 -
"	27		nil.	In addition to usual working parties so men worked on the III Corps dump at LA CHAPELETTE.	L.u.R 23,547 -
"	28		nil.	Working parties as usual.	L.u.R 22,486 -
BUIRE	29		Orders from Inf. Bde to move to BUIRE today.	Bn. moved to BUIRE today starting at 4.15am arriving 2.0pm. Accommodated in Huts.	L.u.R 24,482 - Bde O No.10. L.u.R 24,482.

WAR DIARY
or
INTELLIGENCE SUMMARY.

Army Form C. 2118.

Place	Date	Hour	Summary of Events and Information			Remarks and references to Appendices
	1917.			Strength	total	
	April				24. 482	Bde O N.11
BUIRE.	30.		Bn ordered to move to MILLERS FAUCON. 42 nm relieve 4.8 Bn in the line on 2/5 May.			
			Bn occupied in training in Platoons Bayonet fighting with grenades &c.			
			2.5.17.			
			R.J. Lees. Lt Colonel Cmdg 46th Battalion.			

1577 Wt. W10791/1773 500,000 1/15 D. D. & L. A.D.S.S./Forms/C. 2118.

Vol 4

CONFIDENTIAL.
WAR DIARY
OF.
1/6ᵗʰ BTTN THE LANCASHIRE
FUSILIERS.

FROM. 1.5.17.   TO. 31.5.17.

VOL. N° 22.

WAR DIARY.

MAY 1917.

1/6th Btn. The Lancashire Fusiliers.

VOL 2

Army Form C. 2118.

WAR DIARY
or
INTELLIGENCE SUMMARY.

(Erase heading not required.) 1/6 Batln The Lancashire Fusiliers

VOL. No 22.

Place	Date 1917	Hour	Summary of Events and Information	Remarks and references to Appendices
	MAY			Strength O. O.R.
VILLERS FAUCON. Map Ref. 62c E.29.c.9.	1		Bn marched from BUIRE to VILLERS FAUCON leaving 2.30 p.m., arriving 6.5 p.m. March delayed owing to heavy traffic on the road. Bn. attended by YNCO's in ADRIEN HUTS. Coy Commandant and officers YNCO's visited the line this evening at LEMPIRE.	O. 24. 482 L.W.R.
LEMPIRE F.16.a.9.6.	2		Bn took over from the 11th Lancashire Regt in the line. Bn tea at F.16.a.9.6. front line extends in a semicircle from through F.18.a.6.a. F.6.0.0.7. Relief commenced 9.30 p.m.; working parties 11.30 p.m. Excellent piece of work commenced in the line of posts, large RE working parties digging and connecting up the line of posts. during in front of the line.	24. 482 L.W.R.
"	3		The Bn. to be relieved to the line by the Bn to be relieved by the 11/10 Manchesters next night 4/5 5/15	Posting of importance occurred. Enemy Sniper was active during the day at F.7.6.3.1. He is believed to be located in a hollow tree on or about the spot. He will be shelled and sniped him tomorrow.	24. 484 L.W.R.
"	4			Sniper at F.7.6.3.1. was fired on by 18th Shrapnel likes he used to fire but is thought to be still hurt. During the night patrols went out continuously but did not come into touch with the enemy who is being famine. He continually sends up flares of all colours. No case of this have been reported. No attempt of all Bn. relieved but the Manchester Regt and proceeded to villers FAUCON arriving at 4.15 a.m. 5th inst	24. 529 L.W.R.
VILLERS FAUCON E.22.d.55.	5			300 men on working parties at 12 to 4 am this morning. Other the day in Washing & cleaning. Bn	27. 629 L.W.R.
"	6		Instructions received to relieve 1/7th Manchester Regt in right Support of Div line on the night 8/9 May.	100 men were employed washing at ENNILLE RD during the day & 300 men on the E.B. to ENNILLE RD & RONSSOY ROAD from 8.30 p.m. to 6.45 a.m. 7th inst	27. 643 L.W.R.
"	7			Working parties same as for 6th inst	26. 610 L.W.R.

1577 Wt.W10791/1773 500,000 1/15 D.D.&L. A.D.S.S./Forms/C. 2118.

WAR DIARY
or
INTELLIGENCE SUMMARY.

Army Form C. 2118.

1/6th Bn. Lancashire Fusiliers

Place	Date 1917 May	Hour	Summary of Events and Information Operations			Remarks and references to Appendices
VILLERS FAUCON	8		Bn relieved the 4th Bn Manchester Regt in support totr upon of the Brigade Rector Bn-HQrs at F.1.d.6.4. Bn bivouaced in trenches this Brigade. 2 Coys on working parties of	0. OR 26. 603	wet rained all night	L.H.R
E.22.d.55 EPEHY F.I.d.64	9	nil	Note: Carrying party to R.E. from EPEHY to No.13 Cotne F.3.6.44 Working parties 3 Coys improved digging communication trench all in neighbourhood of LITTLE PRIEL FARM F.4.6.99	26.605	fine	L.H.R
"	10	nil	Working parties same as last night. All light signals are of but working parties down by enemy. Lieut La Kilie F.S.a.19. Shot in air landed F.5.a.19.	26.603	Rain during evening	L.H.R
"	11		Working parties as usual. During the night	26.606	fine	L.H.R
"	12	The Bn relieves the 7. LF in the left light sector of the tomorrow night.	Working parties as usual	25. 601	fine	Bde o.o. No 73. L.H.R
Bn. HQ. No 13 Cope F.3.c.99	13	nil	Bn relieved 7.L.F. in the firing line. Relief commenced at 9pm but was not reported complete until 2.0 am. Bn not going to a frontage being cur(?) to a coy. One coy is on outpost on a line stretching roughly from X.29.6.55. to F.5.d.47. Two companies in the firing line (line of resistance) from X.28. central to F.5.c.75. Enemy very quiet but put up flares continually all night.	26. 594	fine	L.H.R
"	14	nil	Enemy infantry quiet. Shelled LITTLE PRIEL FARM methodically and accurately. No one in there no damage was done. Infantry still quiet.	26. 594	Heavy storm early evening	L.H.R
"	15	nil	Enemy sniper have been fairly active but air not very bad and easy to keep down. LITTLE PRIEL FARM shelled intermittently.	24. 607	fine	L.H.R
"	16	nil	Enemy quiet. Patrols went out during the night but found no evidence of enemy. Enfort occasional bursts of machine fire A.A.10.6. but did no damage.	24. 608	went wet all day	

Army Form C. 2118.

WAR DIARY
or
INTELLIGENCE SUMMARY.
(Erase heading not required.)

1/6th Bn. Lancashire Fusiliers

Instructions regarding War Diaries and Intelligence Summaries are contained in F. S. Regs., Part II. and the Staff Manual respectively. Title pages will be prepared in manuscript.

Place	Date 1917 MAY	Hour	Summary of Events and Information Operations				Remarks and references to Appendices
				Strength	O.R.	Weather	
No 13 COPSE F3-c99.	17		The Bn. is to be relieved by the 2nd only night. Patrols were sent out from our lines 3 times during the night. Enemy not seen in any numbers. Advanced post was found apparently occupied at night. A wire had just been filled with the floor with the Bn. withdrawn so that anyone stepping on the board would disturb the boards. I cannot forward. Bn proceed on to the 30th Divn area.		O.R. 609		Lu.R.
"	18		"	Relief carried out by 16th Lancers and 1 Squadron R.S.W.R Group. Relief commenced at 9.0 pm Completed 2.0 am 18th.	23. 608		Lu.R.
VILLERS FAUCON E.22.a.9.4.	19		"	Bn arrived about 4.0 am. The day spent in cleaning up the men.	24. 629		Qu.R.
EQUANCOURT V.10.a.16 57.c.	20		"	BM marched in Brigade to EQUANCOURT via VILLERS FAUCON 12.40 pm and arrived at 4 pm.	23. 627		Lu.R.
Do.	21		N.L.	Coys under O.C. Coys for training.	21. 597	Fine	Lu.R.
GOUZEAUCOURT WOOD 57.Q.22.c.3.3.	22		The Bn is to relieve the 6th Bn in the VILLERS PLOUCH front Boundaries R.14.d.10 to R.12.b.0.6. Bn in reserve in GOUZEAUCOURT WOOD.	Btn moved from EQUANCOURT to GOUZEAUCOURT WOOD. Time of march 5.7 m. Arrival 9.0 pm. Relief complete 12 midnight. A Coy in Intermediate line R.19.a.55. 1 D Coy to Brown line R.2.c.b.57. B Coy along GOUZEAUCOURT-TRESCAULT Road. C Coy at JHQ.	22. 594	Wet in morning fine afternoon X5.	Lu.R.
"	23		Bttn. ordered to find working parties for Bttns in line at night. A Coy to remain in Brown line of Trench over Brown line Trench.	A Coy commenced digging French Tr.p.b. line in R.P.C. 5.5 " Trench in R 14.d. B Coy was employed in deepening trenches making fire steps in R.7.c 1.9. and R.12.b.3.4. A Coy improved Brown line Trench in Q.28.b.	22. 594	Warm & fine	Lu.R.
"	24		Bttn to relieve the 7th L.F in line night of 25-26th.	All coys carried on work during the night. 600 to 23rd. Swimmer in A Coy received bullet wound in the ankle.	23. 607	Do.	Lu.R.

1577 Wt.W10791/1773 500,000 1/15 D.D. & L. A.D.S.S./Forms/C. 2118.

WAR DIARY or INTELLIGENCE SUMMARY

1/6th Lancashire Fusiliers

Army Form C. 2118.

Place	Date 1917 May.	Hour	Summary of Events and Information OPERATIONS. ORDERS.	STRENGTH O / OR	Weather	Remarks and references to Appendices
GOUZEAUCOURT WOOD 57C. Q.22.c.33	25th		Battn relieved 7th L.F. in the front line (Left Battn). March off 9:30 P.M. Three coys C, B, D, in line A coy with H.Q. Relief completed 2:30 AM 26th. Strength 10:30 P.M. before relief was complete enemy patrol reported on RIBECOURT Rd at R.7.a (Ref.Map 57°C.5E). It was driven off. Flank	0 / 23	Fine	F.F.
In the Line, B⁄Map 57°C.5E. R.13.a.1.7.	26th		coys in touch with 13th W. Yorks on right & 126th Bde on left. The RIBECOURT	22 / 593		App. I. Special report on 2 LT. LEEMINGS Patrol.
do	26th		Road was patrolled for 300 yds in R.7.a. Intense enemy bombardment from 1 AM to 2 AM on VILLERS PLOUICH and our line from R.7.d.07 to R.14.b.30. B.27th, 28th by 2/5 Leicesters. Enemy aircraft party active over our front. Hostile artillery below normal during day. Working party from 1/5 L.F. wiring and digging. Fighting patrol, under 2 Lt LEEMING proceeded in N direction along VILLERS PLOUICH—RIBECOURT road from R.7.d.09. Patrol fired on with rifles from behind when 25" Training. One man missing. (see app. I.) Recon. Battn to be relieved night		Fine	F.F.
do	27th		Battn relieved by 2/5 Leicester Regt. Relief completed. Reconnoitring Patrol at 2:30 AM down road on left of our front. 9/2×16. No trace of enemy found. patrol returned at 3:30 AM. Listening posts out in front of each coy. Nothing to report. Artillery acting (hostile) less than normal. Aerial activity normal. Battⁿ relieved by 1/5th Leicester Regt. Relief completed about 1:30 AM 28th inst. No unusual occurrence	2B / 596		F.F.

Army Form.C. 2118.

WAR DIARY
or
INTELLIGENCE SUMMARY. 1/6th Lancashire Fusiliers

(Erase heading not required.)

Instructions regarding War Diaries and Intelligence Summaries are contained in F. S. Regs., Part II. and the Staff Manual respectively. Title pages will be prepared in manuscript.

Place	Date	Hour	Summary of Events and Information Order / Operations		Strength O / OR	Weather	Remarks and references to Appendices
YPRES. Ref Map. 57C. P.20d.	28th		B/n ordered to parade for inspection by B/n Commander on 31st.	Battn. marched to billets at YPRES. P.20d (Ref 57C) following order. A coy, B coy C coy D coy. Last coy arrived about 4.30 A.M. Afternoon employed in bathing and cleaning up.	O 24	OR 584	Fine	7.F.
do.	29th		Battn ordered to find working party of 400 on 30th with 4 offrs.	Bathing and issue of clean clothes at Divnl Baths Corps in turn. Parades under coy arrangements morning and afternoon	O 25	OR 585	Fine	7.F.
do.	30th			Battn found working party of 400	O 25	OR 585	Fine	7.F.
do.	31st		Battn ordered to find working party of 400 men + 4 officers.	Battn parade at 8.30-9.30 A.M. From 9.30-10.30 AM under coy arrangements. 10.40 AM march on markers for inspection by Brigadier General FRITH. C.B. at 11.00 o'clock. March past in column of route 11.50. Parade under coy arrangements in afternoon	O 25	OR 587		7.F.

1.6.17.

[signature] Major
O/c 1/6th Lanc Fus.

To O.C., C Coy., B.125.   Appx I.

At 10.0 p.m. on the night 26/27 May I proceeded with a patrol of 20 O.R. in a Northerly direction from R.7.d.0.9, where the road running due North from VILLERS PLOUICH crosses the trench occupied by "C" Coy.. The object of the patrol was chiefly to ascertain the unit of the German killed by one of our snipers during the day.

We proceeded in single file until clear of the O.P. on the road. I then took the patrol about 50 yards from the right of the road and formed it into an inverted "V", with the sniper who shot the man as the apex, to act as guide.

In this manner we advanced about 600 yds when we reached a position where the enemy had a salient whose wire was due East of us. We moved forward cautiously for another 70 yards scanning the ground closely, and came across 3 small pits for snipers — they were empty. [I presume that the German was quitting one of these pits, when he was seen & shot by our snipers].

We advanced still further keeping a

close lookout for any trace of the body. My men were then sweeping an area 60 yds broad.

I then observed that 3 Germans were watching us from the crest of the rise on our right, but they took no active measures against us. We continued, therefore, to advance with our right flank resting on his wire; and 40 yards behind the small pits we came across a telephone wire running E. and West. It was about 1/8 inch in diameter, and covered by some coarse black material. Several strands of fine copper wire ran through the centre. We cut it and threw the ends apart.

60 or 70 yards beyond this, the enemy wire turned to a Westerly direction, thus blocking our advance. As no body had been encountered, I came to the conclusion that the body had been removed, so I gave the order to close to the left on to the road.

The 3 men who had been observing us, had followed along parallel to our advance and worked down the slope towards their wire. When they remarked our movement towards the road, they opened fire on us. I therefore doubled my men to the road, and got under the cover of the embankment which was about 6 feet high at that point. I noticed that one of the rifles was being fired from the level of the wire, but whether from a trench or not I could not state.

One rifle at least (and probably two) opened on us from our direct rear as we were moving South along the road. After verifying that all the men were with me, I returned to my trench as quickly as possible. Sporadic fire followed us, but no casualties were occasioned. No machine or Lewis guns opened fire on us.

Ahearn 2/Lt.

By orderly R.O. a.m.,
27 May 1917.

B. 125.

Wire encountered 4yds wide
Rusty red   N Nash Capt

C O N F I D E N T I A L.

War   Diary
of
1/6th. Battalion The Lancashire Fusiliers.

From :-   1st. June, 1917.   To :-   30th. June, 1917.
         (Volume 23).

WAR DIARY or INTELLIGENCE SUMMARY

Army Form C. 2118.

Vol. 23

(Erase heading not required.) 1/6th Batt. The Lancashire Fusiliers

Place	Date	Hour	Summary of Events and Information OPERATIONS / ORDERS	Strength O.	Strength O.R.	Weather	Remarks and references to Appendices
YPRES P.	1.6.17		Entire battn with exception of details employed on working parties	25 12(incl 5 C)	562 321(105 Lrs duty)	Fine and warm.	75
do	2.6.17		Parades from 8.30 AM & 12 noon, all Coys ran experiments for training of Platoon in attack formation, and musketry. 1.30 – 3.30 Coys carried out specialist training.	25	572	ditto	75
ditto	3.6.17		Battn ordered to be at line 728 Bde in line on 5th & 6th inst. Entire battn employed on various working parties. Failure of offs on RFC and communications between Infantry & Artillery by constant patrol work. DNS.	24	581	very warm slight showers	75
do	4.6.17		1/6 L.F. relieved two white 10 Man R. Battn employed on working parties. 2 O.R. per coy sent up to 10th Man in reserve on 5/6/17. Relief to be completed by 5. P.M.	24	575	do	75
HAVRINCOURT WOOD	5.6.17		Nil	Battn parade at 11 A.M. in marching order with iron packs for inspection by C.O. Battn marched from YPRES at 3. P.M. to HAVRINCOURT WOOD. Relieved 10th Man R. Fus reserve. Arrived 4.40 P.M. Relief completed by 5.30 P.M. 2 Coys in intermediate line from is Jenwich 1 coy for 5 minutes, and one coy available for working. 2 Coys with Batt HQ at left reserve 9th L.F. in left sector of front line. No working parties this night	23	575		75
do	6.6.17		Batt'n ordered to find working parties of 200.	1/6 L.F. supplied 4 offs and 176 men to B.E.F. for deepening & widening of communications to the forward posts & extending the posts themselves. Tools drawn at Place mentioned. Distribution Post B. 40 men. Post E. 136. Carrying parties supplied by 9 L.F. work commenced at 10.15 P.M. Approx 18 O.yds of French alos 8 deepened. Bvy had two casualties through bullet wounds. Also supplied three 9 hour shifts of 3 men each to 1st E H.Q. Commenced in at 7 P.M. Hostile artillery quiet.	23	575		Bde Order W/S. W/S 76
do	7.6.17		Nil. Working parties for front line.		23	563		76
do	8.6.17		Nil. B. supplied working parties for first line.		23	562		78, 79

WAR DIARY
or
INTELLIGENCE SUMMARY.

Army Form C. 2118.

(Erase heading not required.)

Vol 23. 1/6 Lancashire Fusiliers

Place	Date	Hour	Summary of Events and Information OPERATIONS / ORDERS	Strength O / OR	Weather	Remarks and references to Appendices
BAREN COURT B	9.6.17		Nil. Bn found working parties for front line. Fourteenth Division		Fine throughout	78
do	10.6.17		Nil. Bn found working parties. Right Half Bn from WIGAN PAVE to CANAL, HRE TRENCH bombing posts southwards. Re-relief of fire steps in trenches.	23 559		76
do	11.6.17		Working parties found for front line.	23 589		75
do	12.6.17		Bn relieved 1/6 Man Bn in front line (orders for relief issued 6th Manchesters OO N°22.) Relief completed. No unusual occurrence. M.G. and T.M. specialists relieved. The resort of the evening relief.	22 604		78
O 7-6-3 & 8.C	13.6.17	Artillery, MGs, TMs bombardment. See 125 Bde Y/6.	Nil. Tension seems apparent in front line improved. Hostile artillery increasingly active. Successful sleep.	22 605		76
do	14.6.17		Two officer patrols left our line at 11 PM. First (8) Returned complete and OR on back at K.33 8.7. Contact attained and some enemy bomb-fire. Patrol returned with 3 OR (1 OR wounded). Bandaged and not accepted. Patrol returned at 11.28 PM. 12 OR. A second patrol (1 Ofr, 10 OR, (H) comprising 8 left, and 15 OR. A contained party K.32 3 5.7 and bomb on enemy's left flank. Patrol reached objective, used bombs and 2L bomber, but did not see any of the enemy. Patrol met with heavy M.G. fire. Patrol returned at 12.15 PM. Reconnaissance HAVRINCOURT and ground beyond was heavily bombarded. No of personal sent at 12 midnight. L.G. Couple couraient mainte in F. post.	22 619		
do	15.6.17	Outpost line to be further consolidated. by 1/8.	Reconnoitring Patrol 1 Ofr, and OR. Left our lines at 11 PM. Bn to accompany N Lancs by FARRINGOOD ALLEY (K.33.d) and passed beyond by R Stoneland about immediately. Enemy. Having failed & reach return, they patrol officers attacked F post, but drove off. Casualties in patrol 1 Ofr killed, three 3 OR wounded. Medium & light T.M were active all night though, also rifle grenades, time completed in front & ground from F. Post in sections post.	22 629		
do	16.6.17		A fighting patrol comprising 1 Ofr, and 30 OR left our lines at 10.30 to ???? MUCKELY BEGINNING through wall & the point when were attacked on both sides rifle fire. After 500 yards of this wounded wall fire Mr. Patrol used hand grenades and were Hot back. The enemy was under cover. I returned at 12 midnight. Thirty grenades and two pistol were expended and were put out. BM. 11.45 PM. 16 Enemy ambushed. D.D.&L. A.D.S.S./Forms/C.2118.	22 616		78

1577 Wt W10791/1773 500,000 1/15 D.D.&L. A.D.S.S./Forms/C.2118.

WAR DIARY
or
INTELLIGENCE SUMMARY.
(Erase heading not required.)

Army Form C. 2118.

Vol 23

1/6th Lancashire Fusiliers

Place	Date	Hour	Summary of Events and Information		Remarks and references to Appendices
			ORDERS	OPERATIONS	
HAVRINCOURT WOOD. G.	17.6.17			Hostile raid on Front line at 12.30 AM (17/6/18) were supported by our 18 pdr's. Enemy in front apparently retired by 1.30 from our front line. Post holding situation intermittently during day. M.G. occasionally used.	Rf
do	18.6.17		Orders as to procedure in case of attack in Ourspot line. 125 Batt. X18/1	Nil. Our activity over party nothing on our front. Coy H.Q. Shelled 2/1/P.M. with near G.post.	604
do	19.6.17		Patrol ordered to K.33.d. 5.7. Vickers and Lewis Guns to be rearranged. 125 Batt. Y.25.	Our artillery was fairly active on our front. The outpost, firing and support lines were shelled considerably during the day. Light and heavy Minnen were continuous active throughout the night. Patrol returned without no positive success owing to bad weather. Trenches were deepened along the outpost line. Road Initica. H & J posts cut across with french. Trenches in most places deep with water, Everything carried on as usual.	Thunderstorm. 22 606
do	20.6.17		Two platoons to meet from Right Reserve Coy into the Old 21st Supports east of Oxford VALLEY. 125 Batt. Y.24.	Hostile activity on Front lines both down in out places. To improve drainage. Constructed using to Enemy fire.	Rainy. 21 604
do	21.6.17		4th East Lancs to relieve 6 E.L.F. O.O. N°2. B.125	Situation Quiet in the line. Battery relieved H.Q. Shelled all day & last 20 Shells dropped close to B.H.Q. Thence did may to continued rain. In relief at night 250 men played in HAVRINCOURT WOOD for work in cable laying. Remainder came by DECAUVILLE Ry. to YTRES Relief complete at 11.15 PM g.22.	Rainy. 22 597
YTRES P	22.6.17		Nil	250 men under Capt Lowsi employed in cable laying in HAVRINCOURT Remainder employed in working parties at ROYAUCOURT and YTRES	Fine 22 608 Rf
do	23.6.17		Nil	Working parties as on previous day	Warm fine 22 602 Rf
do	24.6.17		Nil	Working parties as before	Fine 22 594 Rf
do	24.6.17		Nil	Working parties as before	Fine 22 559 Rf

Army Form C. 2118.

WAR DIARY
or
INTELLIGENCE SUMMARY.

(Erase heading not required.) 1/6th Lancashire Fusiliers

Vol. 23.

Place	Date	Hour	Summary of Events and Information Operations	Orders	Strength O. OR.	Weather	Remarks and references to Appendices
YTRES	26.6.17		Working parties as before. Part of Bn. inoculated (Typhoid + Paratyp. t)	nil	22 . 592	Fine.	RY
do	27.6.17		Working parties as before. Inoculations continue.	nil	22 . 606	Fine.	RY
do	28.6.17		Working parties as before. Inoculations continue.	nil	22 . 610	Fine by day. Thunderstorm at night	RY
do	29.6.17		Working party returned from HAVRINCOURT WOOD after working the day.	nil	22 . 605	Fine.	RY
do	30.6.17		250 men from HAVRINCOURT WOOD inoculated.	Nil	25 . 597	Constant rain all day	RY

Lt Col.
Cmdg B.125.

WAR DIARY.

OF

1/6 BATT. LANCS. FUS.

FOR.

1ST JULY 1917.   31ST JULY/1917

VOL. 24.

WAR DIARY
or
INTELLIGENCE SUMMARY.
(Erase heading not required.)

Army Form C. 2118.

M > A

1/6th Lancashire Fusiliers

Place	Date	Hour	Summary of Events and Information		Strength		Weather	Remarks and references to Appendices
			Orders Operation	Operations	O.	O.R.		
YTRES 57cSE P20d.	1.7.17	-	nil	Firing on range: all companies	24	569	Fine	R.7.
do	2.7.17	-	nil	Company training.	24	570	very warm	R.7.
do	3.7.17	-	nil	Firing on range including Lewis Guns, Live grenade throwing practice.	24	586	Hot	R.7.
do	4.7.17	-	nil	Company training	24	581	Fine and warm	R.7.
do	5.7.17	-	Operation order no.4. Bde to move on 6th from YTRES to GOMIECOURT area via BAPAUME.	Inspection by Lt Col FARGUS a/Brig Gen. 125 Bde. Bde spots in afternoon mounted and flat races.	24	580	Fine Cool	R.7.
GOMIECOURT 57c A22 d	6.7.17	-		Bde marched from YTRES to GOMIECOURT via BAPAUME. Arrived 12.30 p.m. Battalion marched on markers 5.10 a.m. under Canvas.	24	614	Fine Warm	R.7.
"	7.7.17	-		Companies Interior Economy. Competition commenced. Three Coys Inoculated. Arena Visit	24	624	Fine warm.	R.Y.
"	8.7.17	-	G. Training Programme issued for week ending July 15th	Inoculation.	24	627	Thunderstorm & heavy rain	R.4
"	9.7.17	-		Intensive training commenced. Section training in musketry Physical Training, Squad Drill, Rifle exercise; lectures.	24	623	cold	R.4
"	10.7	-		Foot drill in slow time: Communication drill: physical training.	23	624	Fine.	R.M
"	11.7.17	-		One company on the range: others Walking & squad drill. Football in afternoon.	24	665	Warmer.	M
"	12.7.17	-		Specialist training in addition to normal programme. Night work - Digging & strong posts by companies.	24	649	very hot.	M

Army Form C. 2118.

WAR DIARY
INTELLIGENCE SUMMARY.
(Erase heading not required.)

Vol 24 1/6 th Lancashire Fusiliers

Place	Date	Hour	Summary of Events and Information	Orders	Strength O.	Strength O.R.	Weather	Remarks and references to Appendices
GOMMECOURT E7CA22d	13.7.17	-	Coy. and Specialist training. C Coy. on range.	nil	23	651	Fine	RJG
"	14.7.17	-	Bn Route march with Transport via LA COURCELETTE and AYETTE. Left 8 a.m. returned 1 p.m.		23	652	Stormy	RJ.
"	15.7.17	-	Church parade with 5th L.F. Bn Sports. Brigadier opened Sniping Range	Bn Training Programme issued for week ending July 21st	23	650	Fine & warm	RJ.
"	16.7.17	-	Company & Specialist training		21	638	Raining	RJ.
"	17.7.17	-	Company & Specialist training. Bn Mass drill early morning		20	641	Dull warm	RJ.
"	18.7.17	-	Company training. A Coy on range. Field Kitchen Competition held.		20	644	Dull warm	RJ.
"	19.7.17	-	Company training. Bn Mass drill early morning		20	646	Dull Cool wind	RJ.
"	20.7.17	-	Bn drill in early morning. Coy and specialist training. Night work - lifting and wiring a strong post.		20	633	Fine warm	JNS.
"	21.7.17	-	Bn Route march with Transport via CORCELLES, MOYENNEVILLE and HAMELINCOURT. Left 8 a.m., returned 1 p.m. Bde mounted Sports in afternoon	Bn Training Programme issued for week ending July 28th	21	632	Dull & warm	JNS.
"	22.7.17	-	Bde Church parade. Award last May Gen Bde Dismounted Sports.		20	627	Warm & bright	JNS
"	23.7.17	-	Bn Drill. Company training in attack.		20	624	Warm & bright	JNS
"	24.7.17	-	Bn drill. Contact aeroplane Patrol demonstration by 1/8 L.F. Specialist training.		20	627	Very hot	JNS
"	25.7.17	-	Company in attack practice with Smoke grenades		19	626	Close Thunderstorm	JNS
"	26.7.17	-	Bn Drill. Coy & specialist training.		20	618	Fine warm	JNS
"	27.7.17	-	Contact aeroplane patrol practice.		19	626	Very hot	JNS.
"	28.7.17	-	Bn Route march with Transport via COURCELLES, AYETTE, DOUCHY, ABLAINZEVILLE. Left 8am returned 1pm.		17	612	Very hot	JNS.

Army Form C. 2118.

WAR DIARY
or
INTELLIGENCE SUMMARY.
(Erase heading not required.)

V of 24
1/6th Lancashire Fusiliers

Instructions regarding War Diaries and Intelligence Summaries are contained in F. S. Regs., Part II. and the Staff Manual respectively. Title pages will be prepared in manuscript.

Place	Date	Hour	Summary of Events and Information	Remarks and references to Appendices
			ORDERS — OPERATIONS	
GOMMECOURT S/C A22d	29.7.17	—	Programme of training for Week ending Aug 4th issued. Bde Church Parade	
"	30.7.17	—	Coy & Specialist Training. Div Sports.	yes
"	31.7.17	—	Coy Training. Bde Ceremonial Parade.	yes

STRENGTH		WEATHER
O.	O.R.	
17	611	Thunderstorm
17	602	Fine & cool
17	600	Cloudy, close

M.R.H.... Trevor
Cmdg. 1/6 Lan.Fus.

Wt. W10791/1773 500,000 1/15 D. D. & L. A.D.S.S./Forms/C. 2118.
1577

CONFIDENTIAL.

Vol 7

WAR DIARY

of

16th Battn Lancashire Fusiliers.

Vol No 25.

1 August 1917. — 31/8/1917

WAR DIARY
or
INTELLIGENCE SUMMARY.
(Erase heading not required.)

Army Form C. 2118.

Vol. N° 25.

1/6th Lancashire Fusiliers

Place	Date	Hour	Orders	Summary of Events and Information	Strength	Weather	Remarks and references to Appendices
GOMIECOURT S/P A22d	1.8.17	-		MINDEN DAY. On fatigue & training & belt competition with fr		Wet + cold	JSR
"	2.8.17	-		Lectures		Rain	JSR
"	3.8.17	-		Bn attack practice, travel to trench. Coy training in wiring		Showery	JSR
"	4.8.17	-		Bde Route march via COURCELLES, ACHIET LE GRAND, BIHUCOURT, BIEFVILLERS, GREVILLERS, BIHUCOURT, GOMIECOURT 2/Bn returned 12.30 pm		Showery cold	JSR
"	5.8.17	-	Draft Armingt 11/8/17	Church Parade		Fine, bright	JSR
"	6.8.17	-		Bn travel to trench attack practice at LOUPART with live SAA		Fine, mist	JSR
"	7.8.17	-		Coy training, musketry		Dull, showery	JSR
"	8.8.17	-		Bn Route march via COURCELLES, ABLAINZEVILLE, BUCQUOY, ACHIET LE PETIT, ACHIET LE GRAND, COURCELLES. 2/Bn returned 1.15pm		Fine + close Thunderstorm	JSR
"	9.8.17	-		Coy training, attack practice, musketry		Showery	JSR
"	10.8.17	-		Coy training, attack practice, bombing + musketry		Bright, showery	JSR
"	11.8.17	-		Bn travel to trench attack practice with live		Showery	JSR
"	12.8.17	-	Draft Armingt 13/8/17	Church parade		Bright, showery	JSR
"	13.8.17	-		Bn attack practice at LOUPART with live SAA + grenades		Dull, wet	JSR
"	14.8.17	-		Coy specialist training, bombing, musketry		Thunderstorm	JSR

WAR DIARY
or
INTELLIGENCE SUMMARY

(Erase heading not required.)

Army Form C. 2118.

Vol. No. 25

1/6 Lancashire Fusiliers

Instructions regarding War Diaries and Intelligence Summaries are contained in F.S. Regs., Part II. and the Staff Manual respectively. Title pages will be prepared in manuscript.

Place	Date	Hour	ORDERS	OPERATIONS Summary of Events and Information	STRENGTH	WEATHER	Remarks and references to Appendices
GOMIECOURT 57c A22d	15.8.17	—		On Route March with transport via COURCELLES, LOGEAST WOOD, BUCQUOY, ACHIET LE PETIT, ACHIET LE GRAND. Left 8.30am returned 1pm		Showery	JSR
"	16.8.17	—		Ordinary Coy & specialist training. Coy attack practice		Fine, bright	JSR
"	17.8.17	—		Ceremonial drill. Practised to end attack		Fine, hot	JSR
"	18.8.17	—		Bn attack practice 9.00 to 10.30am Assembly, advance under barrage with M.G. & stokes mortar assistance; consolidation of objective.		Fine & warm	JSR
"	19.8.17		Bn ordered to move to BOUZINCOURT			Fine & warm	Op Order No 29/JSR
"	20.8.17	—		Bn moved to BOUZINCOURT via ACHIET LE PETIT, MIRAUMONT, HAMEL, MARTINSART. Started 9am arrived 3.30pm		Fine & hot	JSR
BOUZINCOURT	21.8.17	—	Bn detailed to find party for Coy Training & instructions	Route March (via BLQ) ... 25/8/17 ...		Fine & hot	Op Order 30/JSR Appx 210
"	22.8.17 23.8.17			Amusements ...		Showery	
"	24.8.17					Fine, hot	
"	25.8.17			Draft of 67 other ranks joined ... and Battn paraded ...		Cloudy	
"	26.8.17					Fine & hot	

Army Form C. 2118.

WAR DIARY
INTELLIGENCE SUMMARY
(Erase heading not required.)

Vol I. p. 25.
1/5 Lancashire Fusiliers

Place	Date	Hour	Orders	Summary of Events and Information	[illegible]	Weather	Remarks and references to Appendices
[illegible] L & C 28	27.8.17	—		B.A. & the shelled [illegible] until 10 am. Return to our [illegible] B shellfire reduced to [illegible] & the 27 K 15, 27 [illegible] until [illegible] are due L.K. 11.30 am when 5 cm bomb	[illegible]	[illegible] cold	P.45
"	28.8.17	—	Battalion [illegible] gone to Bde. Res. at [illegible]	B.A. & Shell to [illegible]	[illegible]	Fair rain	Brigade Order No 312
"	29.8.17	—		Battalion marched to [illegible] [illegible] [illegible] at [illegible] & Battn [illegible] Battln. in reserve at 11/6.10.95. [illegible] to [illegible]	[illegible]	Showery	P.45
A & C 28 NW 11.8.10.9.5	30.8.17	—		Continuation of [illegible] from [illegible] at 6 am [illegible] to relieve 7/8th K.O.S.B's. "B", "C" Coys to front line, "A" "D" & HQ at SQUARE FARM	Dull	P.45
Frezenburg C.10.b.29	31.8.17	—	Battn ordered to move back into res. tonight 1-9-17	Relieved 7/8th KOSB by [illegible] [illegible] slightly [illegible] from [illegible] & [illegible] & remainder of day fairly quiet	Showery	P.48 Battn. orders 12.55

Matthew [illegible] Lt. Col.
[illegible] 1/5 Lan Fus.
2/9/17

125/42

CONFIDENTIAL.

WAR DIARY.

OF

1/6th Btn. THE LANCASHIRE FUSILIERS.

FROM. 1.9.17. — 30/9/17   D. 30.9.17.

VOLUME No 26.

WAR DIARY or INTELLIGENCE SUMMARY

Vol: No 26.   Army Form C. 2118.

1/5 Lancashire Fusiliers.

Place	Date	Hour	Summary of Events and Information	Remarks and references to Appendices
Bazentin C.10.b.00 C.10.b.89	1.9.17	Bdr Order 10.57	Day fairly quiet, with exception of Kts or Bns periods of heavy shelling. Battn relief at night by 8th L.F. and Norfolks ("B" Pic Brigade) Battn H.Q. at MILL COTT. Moved by 16th of 1/5 Manchesters for training and were re-	P.Y.S.
Dul C.28.N.W. 1/10,000 1/5 a 78	2.9.17		located by 16th of 1/5 Manchesters.	P.Y.S.
	3.9.17		Spent day improving bivouacs; carrying parties supplied at night to R.E.'s, D Coy, (half "B" Coy) for training.	P.Y.S.
do	8.9.17		Some work during the day on trenches; carrying parties supplied at night.	P.Y.S.
	4.9.17 5.9.17	Brigade Order 13.9.17	Battalion relieved 8th L.F. in the line. Relief without incident 3/9/17. Very heavy barrage took place about 9 p.m. for about an hour, which appeared to be the enemy about to attack on the following day with a view to retake hill 60 and carrying parties knocked out.	
	6.9.19.	Splinter Order for do.	Battalion attacked enemy position at Breakthorn Seagrand Lines N.S., a "B" "C" "D" Coys, A Coy in Support to heavy M.G. fire and an expected night artillery "B" Battalion "A" advanced before they consolidated during the attack.	
	7.9.17		Fairly quiet day; Battalion relieved at night by 8th Manchesters Marched back to Ypres, then travelled back to rest camp where parade in afternoon.	P.Y.S.
huts 78 aux 72	8.9.17			P.Y.S.
do	9.9.17		Divine Service in morning; clothing parades	
do	10.9.17		bay.: specialist training; pay parade + organized games.	P.Y.S.

WAR DIARY

INTELLIGENCE SUMMARY.

Vol: No: 26.
1/6th Lancashire Fusiliers.

Army Form ... 18.

(Erase heading not required.)

Instructions regarding War Diaries and Intelligence Summaries are contained in F.S. Regs., Part II. and the Staff Manual respectively. Title pages will be prepared in manuscript.

Place	Date	Hour	Orders	Operations. Summary of Events and Information	Strength.	Weather.	Remarks and references to Appendices
Week 28 a.11.c.7.2.	11/9/17			Coy & Specialist training in morning; organised games in afternoon.		Fine.	p.243.
do:	12/9/17			Coy + Specialist training.		Fine.	p.243.
do:	13/9/17			do:		Fine.	p.243.
do:	14/9/17		Batta: order No 37	Battalion moved up at night into support line: Hdqrs: at Huit Batti Relief completed at 11d.m. A + B forming V.116 of strength, and C + D forming N.2 Coy on L/C.		do.	p.243.
Sheet 28 N.W. 1/40000 L.3.a.2.8.	15/9/17			Day spent improving trenches, working parties at night.		do.	p.243.
do:	16/9/17		Batta: order No 38	do:		do.	p.243.
do:	17/9/17			Batt: relieved at night by 27th South African Infantry Bgd:, and marched back to G.11.c.9.2., arriving there about 3 a.m.		do.	p.243.
Week 28 a.11.c.7.2.	18/9/17			Day spent at inspections &c: no further parades &c: bol: stamped hird Meda Battn: old command fallen over by Lieut: Colonel Thorpe D.S.O.		do.	p.243.
Sheet 27 N.E. L.3. Central.	19/9/17		Batta: order No 39	Battalion attached for Bivouac (Sheet 27 N.E. approx: L.3.Central.)		do.	p.243.
do:	20/9/17			Coy + Specialist training. Bathing parades.		do.	p.243.

Army Form C. 2118.

WAR DIARY
INTELLIGENCE SUMMARY.
(Erase heading not required.)

VOL: No: 26.
1/6th Lancashire Fusiliers

Instructions regarding War Diaries and Intelligence Summaries are contained in F. S. Regs., Part II. and the Staff Manual respectively. Title pages will be prepared in manuscript.

Place	Date	Hour	Summary of Events and Information		Remarks and references to Appendices
			Orders.	Operations.	
Huts 7 N.E. L.B.C. pital	26/9/17			Coy: & Specialist training.	Weather: Fine. P.W.S.
do:	27/9/17		Bde:order No 40	Batln: landed at 2.45 p.m. and marched to entraining point at Steenvoorde. Thence by train to arriving at about 11 p.m. Batln: in billets.	Fine. P.W.S.
HAZEBROUCK 5.A.	28/9/17			No parade; men resting.	do: P.W.S.
do:	29/9/17		Bde:order No 41	Batln: paraded at 6 a.m. and marched to entraining point at Hazebrouck; thence by train to [?]. Shoulder planning about 9.45 a.m.	Fine shot. P.W.S.
Huts 19 D 22.	30/9/17		Bde: order No 42	Batln: landed at 1.15 p.m. and marched to Huts 115.E.W.11.C. central. Batln: in huts. (Arrived about 5.30 p.m.)	do: P.W.S.
Huts 115.E. W.11.c. central.	1/10/17			Coy: & Specialist training. Nothing particular.	do. P.W.S.
do:	2/10/17			Batln: on duty; fatigue parties found thro' remainder training.	do. P.W.S.
do:	3/10/17			Coy: & Specialist training, that is, parades.	do: P.W.S.
do:	4/10/17			Batln: Route march. Paraded at 8.15 a.m. Returned 11.45 a.m. Organised games in afternoon.	do: P.W.S.
do:	5/10/17			Church Parade.	do. P.W.S.

D. Shephard
Comdg 1/6 Lancs Fus.

CONFIDENTIAL.

War   Diary

of

1/6th Battalion The Lancashire Fusiliers.

From 1.10.17.   To 31.10.17.

Volume No 27.

COPY 7, 11, 11, 11, 12, 14

Army Form C. 2118.

WAR DIARY
~~INTELLIGENCE~~ SUMMARY.
(Erase heading not required.)

VOL: No 27
1/6 Lancashire Fusiliers

Instructions regarding War Diaries and Intelligence Summaries are contained in F.S. Regs., Part II. and the Staff Manual respectively. Title pages will be prepared in manuscript.

Place	Date	Hour	Orders	Summary of Events and Information	Strength	Weather	Remarks and references to Appendices
Sheet 11 SE W11 C Central	1/10/17			Coy specialist training in morning. Organized games in the afternoon.		Fine Warm.	A/J.H.
-do-	2/10/17			Coy specialist training; during the morning the Battn was given a demonstration of 3" mortar shells for day signalling. Organized games in afternoon; special class for N.C.O's.		Fine Calm	A/J.H.
-do-	3/10/17			Working Party 1 officer 56pR applied to relieve similar party of 7th Lancs. Fus. at SURREY CAMP R32 B56. Sh: 11 SE. Working Party 180 who hrs to work at R 33 D 6.5.		Dull Misty	A/J.H.
-do-	4/10/17			Cleaning equipment.		Cool. Very windy	A/J.H.
-do-	5/10/17			March from Aldebolde (M11 Central) to relieve 11th Border Regt and take over left sector of Brigade Front Sheet 5 M22 c+d; M28 a+c+d. Newport area. Relief was effected without casualties		Not Cloudy	A/J.H.
Sheet 5 N28 Central	6/10/17			In Trenches: repairs & improvements carried out. In the evening several casualties in Bng out thro enemy direct hit. Enemy artillery fairly active.		Rain Mist Changeable.	A/J.H.

1577 Wt. W10791/1773 500,000 1/15 D.D.&L. A.D.S.S./Forms/C. 2118.

WAR DIARY
INTELLIGENCE SUMMARY

VOL 27
1/6th Lancashire Fusiliers

Army Form C. 2118.

Place	Date	Hour	Orders	Operations / Summary of Events and Information	Strength	Weather	Remarks and references to Appendices
Sheet 5 M 28 Central	7.10.17			In the trenches. Enemy Artillery fairly active.		Rain + mist. Changeable	60/52
do	8.10.17			do		Dull + misty	60/52
do	9.10.17			do Relieved at night by 8th Lancs Fuslrs took over the NEWPORT SECTOR SHEETS M 28 C+D also M 21 D Y M 27 B. The Bn were relieved without Bn casualties.		Fine day rain at night.	60/52
do	10.10.17			In Reserve. Working parties supplied 6 RE carrying etc.		Showery	60/52
do	11.10.17			do		Fine + cold	60/52
do	12.10.17			do		Showery Hail	60/52
do	13.10.17	Op. Ord. 123		Relieved the 8th Lancs Fuslrs at M22 C+D, M28 a.b.c.d. Relief was effected without casualties.		Dull, showery	60/52
do	14.10.17			In the trenches. General work at improvement to Enemy Artillery fairly active.			
do	15.10.17			-do-			
do	16.10.17			-do-			
do	17.10.17	Op. Ord. 124		Bn Relieved at night by 8th Lancs Fuslrs took over NEWPORT SECTOR Sh.5 M 28 C+D also M 21 D r M 27 B. No casualties during relief.		Fine	60/52
do	18.10.17			In Reserve. Cleaning up equipment etc.		Fine	60/52

WAR DIARY

Army Form C. 2118.

VOL 27

INTELLIGENCE SUMMARY

1/6th Lancashire Fusiliers

Place	Date	Hour	Orders	Summary of Events and Information	Strength	Weather	Remarks and references to Appendices
NEWPORT SECTOR SH.5 M28c x 9 & M21a M27	19.10.17		opord 125	In reserve. Demo gun positions for AA work shelled by enemy.		Fine	h/JX
do	20.10.17		opord 126	do Lewis gun post blown in by direct ht. several casualties relieved at night by 6 Manchr Regt. No casualties down relief: about 20 gas shells were sent over by enemy during the relief but had no effect. On marched to Australia Camp. Co x 9 D.E. Sh.11 SE x 13 b.		Fine	h/JX
SH 11SE x 13 b	21.10.17			Cleaning up. In the afternoon the Bn marched to La PANNE & went into billets in N.15 a.		Fine	h/JX
Sh 11 SE N 15 a	22.10.17			Cleaning up & changing clothing: general refitting. Company pay day.		Fine	h/JX
do	23.10.17			Lectures & Company arrangements. Musketry & Indoor training.		Very wet	h/JX
do	24.10.17			Platoon & Company drill; musketry & P.J. games.		Changeable	h/JX
do	25.10.17			a draft of 157 arrived in the afternoon from 229th I.R. Rettn. Company arrangements: lectures & indoor training		Fine but very changeable at noon	h/JX
do	26.10.17			Company arrangements. Range Practice: Bathing Parade in afternoon.		Fine	h/JX
do	27.10.17			Drill & musketry: Draft inspected by Divisional Commander. P.O.C. 42 Bn.		Fine	h/JX
do	28.10.17			Church Parade in Morning. Organized games in afternoon		Fine, cold	h/JX
do	29.10.17		opord 127 & 128	Marched to Boryde (Australia Camp) Sh.11 SE x 13 b taking over from 8th Lanc Fus. Working Party to Officers 100.OR enfiled to Dir.P.6 dump.		-"- -"-	h/JX

Army Form C. 2118.

WAR DIARY

INTELLIGENCE SUMMARY

VOL 27
16th Lancashire Fusiliers

(Erase heading not required.)

Place	Date	Hour	Summary of Events and Information	Remarks and references to Appendices
			orders / operation / Strength / Weather	
S.11 SE 13.6	30.10.17		Working Parties. 3 Officers 186 O.R. + 2 Officers 100 O.R. supplied by Bn. Remainder of Bn under Company Specialist Training.	Very cloudy dull cold — C/52
do	31.10.17		Working Party of 150 O.R. supplied by Bn. Remainder of Bn on Tactical Scheme under C.O. also Specialist Training & games in afternoon	Fine — C/52

Jno. Keith Mentath
Major
Cmdg 16 Lan Fus

I.O.

SECRET.   COPY No. 7

BATTALION ORDER No. 125.

BATTALION IN RESERVE.

Reference Map $\frac{1}{10.000}$ No. 5.

1. The Defence of the Front Line is carried out by the 2 Front Line Battalions each of which have one Company available for counter-attack.

2. In addition the Support Battalion has one Company ready for immediate counter-attack if necessary.

3. The Reserve Battalion is under the immediate orders of the Brigade.

4. In case of an attack by night working parties of the Reserve Battalion H.Q. will report to the nearest Battalion or Company H.Q.

   By day they will ~~XXXXX~~ rejoin their own Companies with the least possible delay.

19.10.17.

Issued, by Orderly, at 1.0 p.m.

                                                    R.E. Robinson
                                                    Captain,
                                       Adjutant, 1/6th Lan. Fus.

Distribution:-

    Copy No. 1.   C.O.
      "   2.   2/in Command.
      "   3.   O.C. A. Company.
      "   4.   "   B.   "
      "   5.   "   C.   "
      "   6.   "   D.   "
      "   7.   M.D. ✓
      "   8.   File.
      "   9.   For handing over.

SECRET.   1/6th LANCASHIRE FUSILIERS.   COPY No. 11

BATTALION OPERATION ORDER No. 123. 12.10.17.

Reference Map $\frac{1}{10,000}$ Sheet 5.

1. The Battalion will relieve 8th Lan. Fus. in Left sub-sector of Brigade Front on night 13/14th October.
7th Lan. Fus. will be in support, 8th Lan. Fus. in reserve.

2. Companies and platoons will take over the same trenches and posts that were occupied during the last tour.

3. Head of each Company will reach CROWDER BRIDGE in the following order:-

        C. Company.   9.30 p.m.
        B.   "   9.45 p.m.
        H. Q.   9.50 p.m.
        A. Company.   10.0 p.m.
        D.   "   10.15 p.m.

No Guides will be provided.
O.C. Coys will carefully reconnoitre route to CROWDER BRIDGE before leaving.

4. 2 days rations have been drawn to-day- One days rations will be carried up to the Line on the man. Water bottles will be filled before leaving.

5. Men's feet will be rubbed to-morrow with whale oil before going up. Clothing will also be treated with anti-vermin grease. A Certificate that this has been done will be rendered by O.C. Coys by 7.0 p.m. to-morrow.

6. Sgt. Chadwick will proceed to INDIARUBBER HOUSE by 4.0 p.m. to-morrow to be ready to take over signals.

7. Acknowledge

8. Relief complete will be reported by Runner.

Issued, by orderly, at 9.0 am 13/10/17
AB1/792.

                                     L.E.Robinson
                                            Captain,
                                     Adjutant, 1/6th Lan. Fus.

Distribution:-

Copy No. 1   C.O.
"   2   2/in Command.
"   3   O.C. A. Company.
"   4   "   B.   "
"   5   "   C.   "
"   6   "   D.   "
"   7. Lieut. Barker.
"   8   Quartermaster.
"   9   Transport Officer.
"   10   Sgt. Chadwick.
"   11   W. D.
"   12   File.
"   13   Spare.
"   14   Adjutant.

SECRET.   COPY No. 11

BATTALION MARCHING ORDER No. 122.

The 6th Lancashire Fusiliers will move to GOAYDE on
the 29th October, taking over from the 6th Lancashire Fusiliers

                                      L. Robinson
                                                 Captain,
                                      Adjutant, 1/6th Lan. Fus.

Distribution:-
Copy No. 1 O.C.
"   "   2 2/in Command.
"   "   3 O.C. A Company.
"   "   4   "   B   "
"   "   5   "   C   "
"   "   6   "   D   "
"   "   7 Quartermaster.
"   "   8 Transport Officer.   Issued by orderly at _____ hrs.
"   "   9 Medical Officer.   26.10.17.
"   " 10 File.
"   " 11 W.D.
"   " 12 Spare.

SECRET.   COPY No. 11

                        1/6th Lancashire Fusiliers.
              BATTALION OPERATION ORDER No. 128.

Reference Map 1:40.000 FORNES.
1.   6th Lancashire Fusiliers will move to AUSTRALIA CAMP to-morrow, and
     take over from 8th Lancashire Fusiliers.
2.   March on markers 9.45 a.m.   Companies will fall in, in line, A Coy
     on left facing the buildings. DRESS:- Marching order, steel helmets.
3.   Companies will move at 20 x distance.   Transport will move in the
     rear of the Battalion with usual distances between groups of vehicles.
4.   Billeting party under Lieut. J. S. Barker, consisting of C.Q.M.S. of
     each Company, and Sgt. Chadwick for Battalion H.Q., will parade at Bttn.
     H.Q. at 8.45 a.m. and proceed in advance.
5.   All baggage to be stacked near the Q.M's Stores by 8.30 a.m.
6.   Orders re the relief of working parties now found by the 6th Lancashire
     Fusiliers will be issued separately.

                                                          L.Robinson
                                                                    Captain,
Issued by Orderly at 1-30 p.m.   Adjutant, 1/6th Lan. Fus.
Distribution:
Copy No. 1   C.O.
  "   " 2   O.C. A. Company.
  "   " 3   "   B.   "
  "   " 4   "   C.   "
  "   " 5   "   D.   "
  "   " 6   Medical Officer.
  "   " 7   Quartermaster.
  "   " 8   Transport Officer.
  "   " 9   Lieut. J. S. Barker.
  "   " 10   R.S.M.
  "   " 11   War Diary.
  "   " 12   File.
  "   " 13   Spare.

L.B.

SECRET.　　　　　　　　　　　　　　　　　　　　　　　　COPY No. 12

1/6th LANCASHIRE FUSILIERS.

BATTALION OPERATION ORDER No. 124.　　　16.10.17.

Reference Map $\frac{1}{10,000}$ No. 5.

1. 8th Lancashire Fusiliers will relieve 6th Lancashire Fusiliers in left Subsector of Brigade Front to-morrow night 17/18th October.
6th Lan. Fus. will move into Brigade Reserve.
7th Lan. Fus. will relieve 5th Lan. Fus. in right Subsector.

2. Companies on relieve will move via PUTNEY BRIDGE to the same billets occupied by them before.　　O.C. Coys will call at Battalion H.Q's when passing and report relief.　　Arrival in billets will be reported by wire to new Battalion H. Q's by code word "YORK".

3. 2/Lieut. S. P. Cooling will proceed in advance to arrive at 8th Lan. Fus. H. Q's at 3.0 p.m. 17th October, and take over all stores, documents, and Lewis Gun Mountings etc.

4. Rations for 18th October will be drawn and issued at Billets on 17th/18th October.

5. All trench stores, maps, aeroplane photographs, etc., will be handed over and receipts obtained, copies of which will be forwarded to Battalion H. Q's by 10.0 a.m. 18th instant.

6. O.C. D. Company will detail an Officer and 6 men to report to Bridge Officer INDIARUBBER HOUSE at 4.0 p.m. 17th October.

7. No Guides will be provided.

8. ACKNOWLEDGE.

Issued, by Orderly, at _____ p.m.　　　　　　L. Robinson.
　　　　　　　　　　　　　　　　　　　　　　　　　　　　　　Captain,
　　　　　　　　　　　　　　　　　　　　Adjutant, 1/6th Lan. Fus.

Distribution:-
Copy No.　1　C. O.
 "　　　2　2/in Command.
 "　　　3　O.C. A. Company.
 "　　　4　 " B.   "
 "　　　5　 " C.   "
 "　　　6　 " D.   "
 "　　　7　Quartermaster.
 "　　　8　Transport Officer.
 "　　　9　2/Lieut. Cooling.
 "　　 10　Bridge Control Officer.
 "　　 11　8th Lan. Fus.
 "　　 12　W. D.
 "　　 13　R. S. M.
 "　　 14　Spare.
 "　　 15　File.

L.B.

SECRET.   COPY No. 1-2

BATTALION OPERATION ORDER No. 12.
(1/6th Lan. Fus.)

Reference Map 1:10.000 Sheet 5.
"   "   1:40.000 NIEUPRE Sheet.

1. 6th Lan. Fus. will be relieved by 6th Man. Regt. on night 20/21st October. Head of 6th Man. Regt. will reach PELICAN BRIDGE by 7.0 p.m.

2. On relief 6th Lan. Fus. will move to COXYDE, and to LA PANNE on the 21st.

3. Billeting party under Lieut. J. S. Barker will meet Rear Staff Captain on 20th October, at WHITE HOUSE, GINASA CAMP, at 10.30 a.m. and on the 21st October at Cross Roads (T. 20 b. 95) South of La Panne at 10.0 a.m.

4. 4 Guides per Company will report to Adjutant at 4.0 p.m. to-day. (1 per Company H. Q. and 3 for platoons). They must be intelligent men and must know the way from their Company to ARCH BRIDGE, if possible to PELICAN BRIDGE. They will be under charge of 2/Lieut. J. W. King who will also report to Adjutant at 4.0 p.m. for instructions.

5. Arrangements for transport are as follows:-
Limbers are coming to ARCH BRIDGE at intervals of about ½ hour during the afternoon from 1.0 p.m. A. C. and D. Coys will send their men's packs there during the morning and dump them there under 1 man per Coy who will load them on to Limbers and who accompany the packs to COXYDE, where they will be off-loaded in new Company Lines.
Packs must be sent down by small bodies of men and tunnels and trenches used whenever possible.
B. Company will send packs to same place after dusk. Lewis Gun Limbers will be at ARCH BRIDGE at 9.0 p.m. and Coys will load on to these as they pass, leaving a man to accompany each Limber.

6. On relief each Company will march to COXYDE via ARCH BRIDGE-ZOUAVE track (to main OOST DUNKERK- NIEUPORT Road) -OOST DUNKERK- COXYDE.
100ᵡ distance between platoons

7. Relief complete will be reported by wire, by Code word "BEER".

8. On relief all Trench Stores, S.A.A., Grenades, etc., Maps, photographs Defence Schemes, etc., will be handed over. Receipts obtained for these will be sent to Adjutant by 10.0 a.m. 21st October.

9. 6 A.A. Lewis Guns (less sights and mountings) will be taken over from 6th Man. Regt. in the COXYDE area on 21st October. The L. G. Officer of 6th Man. Regt. will report to 2/Lieut. Cooling at 9.0 a.m. 21st October to arrange details of relief. 2/Lieut. Cooling will arrange for teams to be ready to move at this hour. They will have 1 day's rations. Each pair of guns will be under charge of an Officer. 2/Lt. Sutherland and 2/Lt. Evans will report to 2/Lieut. Cooling at 9.0 a.m. 21st October for this duty.
These guns will be relieved by 8th L. F. on 22nd October- teams will then join the Battalion at LA PANNE.

10. ACKNOWLEDGE.

20.10.17.

Issued, by orderly, at 1.0 p.m.

L. Robinson
Captain,
Adjutant, 1/6th Lan. Fus.

Distribution-
Copy No. 1. C.O.   9. 2/Lt. Cooling
"   "   2. 2/in Command.   10. "   King.
"   "   3. A. Coy.   11. Transport Officer.
"   "   4. B. "   12. 2/Lt. Sutherland.
"   "   5. C. "   13. "   Evans.
"   "   6. D. "   14. War Diary. ✓
"   "   7. Quartermaster.   15. File.
"   "   8. Lt. Barker.   16. R.S.M.

CONFIDENTIAL:

1/6th Lancashire Fusiliers

WAR DIARY.
Vol. 28.   November 1917.

1/11/1917 — 30/11/1917

WAR DIARY
INTELLIGENCE SUMMARY
(Erase heading not required.)

Army Form C. 2118.

VOL: 28

1/6th Lancashire Fusiliers

Instructions regarding War Diaries and Intelligence Summaries are contained in F.S. Regs., Part II. and the Staff Manual respectively. Title pages will be prepared in manuscript.

Place	Hour, Date, Place Date	Orders	Summary of Events and Information	Strength Officers	OR	Remarks weather	Remarks and references to Appendices
Place Sh.IISE.X.13b	1.11.1917		Australia Camp, Coxyde. Tactical Schemes, Specialist training. 4 Officers, 250 Other Ranks on Working Parties.	9	550	Fine. Cold	60/72
do	2.11.1917		ditto. Tactical Schemes, Specialist Training. 4 Officers, 179 Other Ranks on Working Parties.	14	548	Fine. do	60/72
do	3.11.1917		ditto. Specialist Training. 5 Officers, 238 Other Ranks on Working Parties.	13	557	Misty. 2wire	60/72
do	4.11.1917		ditto. Specialist Training. 5 Officers, 207 Other Ranks on Working Parties.	13	560	Fine. Cold	60/72
do	5.11.1917		Interior economy. Special Training. 2 Officers, 51 OR on Working Parties.	14	567	Fine. Bright	60/72
do	6.11.1917	Op. Ord. 130	Bn marched to Newport 5 where 6th Wilcher's Regt in left front of Regt about Kn 22 & Kn 28 21.5. During the morning, Interior Economy.	19	589	Hot & Cold	60/72
Sh.5. N.22. 8.28	7.11.1917		In Trenches. Repairs & improvements carried out. Desultory shelling by enemy. 73 men on working parties.	19	592	Fine	60/72
do	8.11.17		In Trenches. Usual desultory shelling by enemy. Our Patrols out. 85 OR by night. 360 day working parties.	19	593	Fine	60/72
do	9.11.17	Op. Ord. 131	In Trenches. Bn H.Q. heavily shelled. 66 OR working parties.	20	593	Fine	60/72
do	10.11.17		In Trenches. Relieved at night by 8th Bn Lancs Fus. No casualties during relief. working party supplied of 25 OR.	20	595	Dull	60/72

WAR DIARY or INTELLIGENCE SUMMARY

Army Form C. 2118.

VOL 28.
1/6th Lancashire Fusiliers

Place	Hour, Date	Place orders	Summary of Events and Information	Strength O.R.	Remarks weather	References to Appendices Remarks
Place. 25.M.28	11.11.17		In Reserve in Brigade in MALLANO in NIEUPORT & M.20.C. & N.17.B. M.7.B. Working parties supplied	20 596	Fine	C/JR.
do	12.11.17		do Resting & cleaning up. Working parties supplied. do	20 600	Misty	C/JR.
do	13.11.17		do Repairs to PRESQUILE trenches. do	18 596	Fine	C/JR.
do	14.11.17	op ord. 132	do at night relieved the 8th L.F. in M22 & M28 Jo-lambattns.	18 591	Dull muggy	C/JR.
do	15.11.17		In trenches. Usual shelling by enemy. Night patrolling. Companies in the line repairing & improving trenches	17 585	Fine	C/JR.
do	16.11.17		do do do	19 584	Fine	C/JR.
do	17.11.17		do do do	20 589	Misty	C/JR.
do	18.11.17	op ord 133	In trenches. Relieved at night by 6th Bn 321 French Inf. Regt. Relief carried out without Bn casualties. The Bn marched to OOST DUNKERQUE & went into billets for the remainder of the night. C Company under 2nd Lt 17th R Ryle accommodated in BRISBANE CAMP	20 589	Clear cold	C/JR.
OOST-DUNKERQUE Str. 150–160 200 M.11V19 M horses	19.11.17 400 OR	op ord 134	Batt. marched to TETEGHEM area. Route via LAMPNE–ADINKERKE–POINT–DEZOYDCOTE thence LEFFRINGOUCKE–UXEM. transport starting point cross road W18 c 6.7. Batt was billeted in UXEM & vicinity.	21 588	Fine	C/JR.
St 5,19 27 400 or 10.11.17		op ord. 135	Batt. marched to NORMHOUDT "A" area. Route via L4 MYNNE Starting from road junction Z8 a 8.4 Route des MOERES-NOYELLE — eastern outskirts of BERGUES – FAVES – -HE-CASSEL – NORMHOUDT. Battalion billeted in NORMHOUDT "A" area	21 590	Fine	C/JR.
Sh. 27 ½ 40-80	21.11.17	op ord: 136	Batt. marched to WARNERS-CAPPEL. Route KIEKEN-POT cross roads 500 yards NNE HARDIPORT – L'ANGE – WARNERS-CAPPEL. Billets at last place.	21 600	Fine	C/JR.
Sh. 27 ½ 40-80	22.11.17	op ord. 137	Batt. marched to WALLON-CAPPEL & STAPLE area. Route ZUYTPEENE–MULSE-HOUCK–LES TROIS ROIS. Billeted in STAPLE area.	23 601	Misty	C/JR.

WAR DIARY *or* **INTELLIGENCE SUMMARY.**
(Erase heading not required.)

Army Form C. 2118.

VOL. 28.
1/6th Lancashire Fusiliers

Place	Hour, Date	Orders	Summary of Events and Information	Trench O.R.	Strength	Remarks and references to Appendices
Place to 22.11.17 to 30.11.17	22.11.17	Opord 138	Battn marched to THIENNES. Route by the Ronian Road. Resting in afternoon, in Billets.	22	596	Weather Fine — Appx.
THIENNES	24.11.17		In billets at THIENNES. Interior economy + Company arrangements for training in morning. Organised games in afternoon.	23	602	Fine/Cold. Appx.
do	25.11.17		In billets at THIENNES. Hot baths arranged in old Brewery. Voluntary Church Parade in morning.	23	603	Fine/Cold windy. Appx.
do	26.11.17		In billets at THIENNES. Company Arrangements cleaning up. C. Coy rejoined from NIEUPORT return.	24	604	Changeable Cold. Appx.
do	27.11.17	B.N.Op Ordr No 139	March to BETHUNE area via CROIX MARRHISSE - ST VENANT - ROBECQ. Billets in OBLINGHEM.	25	593	Rain. J.B.S.
OBLINGHEM (Ref 36a) V.29	28.11.17	B.N.Op.Ordr No140	March to relieve 8th Border Regt in support near GIVENCHY, via BETHUNE, BEUVRY, and LE PREOL. Transport at LEQUESNOY. Very little activity in line; no casualties during relief	25	596	Fine + bright J.B.S.
GIVENCHY (Ref 36c a/8c)	29.11.17		Day working parties! repairs to trenches; construction of dug-outs. Increased artillery activity.	24	597	Fine + cold J.B.S.
do	30.11.17		Day working parties trench improvements. Part of Bn visited baths at LE PREOL. Increased shelling in afternoon + evening.	23	577	Fine; showy J.B.S

E. Shorpham Lt. Col.
Commanding 1/6 Lancs Fus.

CONFIDENTIAL.

WAR DIARY

of

1/6th Battalion The Lancashire Fusiliers.

From ~~XXIX~~ 1.12.17............To 31.12.17.

Volume No. 29.

APP 1, 2, 3, 4, 5, 6, 7, 8

WAR DIARY
INTELLIGENCE SUMMARY.
(Erase heading not required.)

Army Form C. 2118.

VOL 29.
1/6th LANCASHIRE FUSILIERS.

Place	Hour, Date, Place Date Orders	Summary of Events and Information	Strength O. OR.	Remarks and references to Appendices Weather	Remarks
GIVENCHY (Maps 36c A & c)	1.12.17	Working parties on R.E. work. Trench maintenance. Very little activity.		Cold & dull. Showers.	JSS
"	2.12.17	T.M. fire on right sector during afternoon. Working parties for R.E.		Cold & bright	JSS
"	3.12.17	Little enemy activity. Working parties for R.E. Trench maintenance.		Cold & bright	JR
CUINCHY (Map 36c A.15)	4.12.17	18:00 Oct 14. We relieved 1/8th L.F. in firing line, A, D, & C Coys in front line; B Coy in support. Relief started at 9 am, finished by 12 noon; no casualties. Little enemy activity.		Cold & bright Ref App 1.	JKS
"	5.12.17	Increased enemy artillery & T.M. fire during day; trenches damaged in a few places.		Cold & bright.	JR
"	6.12.17	In trenches. Normal routine: Patrols & repairing of trenches		do	WR
"	7.12.17	do do Patrols do		do	WR
"	8.12.17	do do do		Cold & misty	WR
"	9.12.17	do do do		All day rain.	WR

WAR DIARY or INTELLIGENCE SUMMARY

Army Form C. 2118.

VOL 29
1/6th LANCASHIRE FUSILIERS

Place	Hour, Date	Orders	Summary of Events and Information	Weather	Remarks and references to Appendices
QUINCHY MAP 36C A-15	10.12.17	B.R.O. 142/143	Battalion relieved in the morning by 1/10 Manchester Regt. & marched to BETHUNE & billetted in TOBACCO FACTORY ref. BETHUNE MAP 1.40000 E17.8.9.9. afternoon cleaning up.	Bright or Bright	6/9/2 ref App. 2.3.4.5.
BETHUNE 1.40000. E17.9.0.9.	11.12.17		Resting. Cleaning up & refitting.	do	6/9/2
do	12.12.17		Company arrangements & Interior economy. Games organized in afternoon.	do	6/9/2
do	13.12.17		Company training; Musketry, Bombing etc by Specialists organized games in afternoon.	do	6/9/2
do	14.12.17		ditto	cold	6/9/2
do	15.12.17		ditto	misty & cold	6/9/2
do	16.12.17		Divine Service in morning in the Open in followed by presentation of ribbons for honours by the Divisional Commander. Holiday in afternoon.	Bright & cold	6/9/2
do	17.12.17		Company Training Specialist Training, Musketry, Bombing, Lewis Gun. Organized exercises & games in afternoon by Companies.	very frosty	6/9/2
do	18.12.17		ditto	do	6/9/2
do	19.12.17		ditto	do	6/9/2
do	20.12.17		ditto	do	6/9/2
do	21.12.17		ditto	do	6/9/2

WAR DIARY or INTELLIGENCE SUMMARY.

Army Form C. 2118.

(Erase heading not required.)

VOL 29

1/6 LANCASHIRE FUSILIERS

Place	Hour, Date		Summary of Events and Information	Remarks and references to Appendices
RUE	SOUND			Weather
PETHUNE 1 My 100	22.12.17	BR0 145	Battalion marched to GORRE F=36.6.5 to relieve 1/5 Man.Regt. in Reserve. Route via LE QUESNOY	Frosty. Bright. 6/01 Ref. Off. 6
GORRE F3.6.55	23.12.17		Company arrangements training in morning Games in afternoon	do 6/01
do	24.12.17		Company arrangements Rehearsal of training in morning	do 6/01
do	25.12.17		Christmas Day Holiday	Snow 6/01
do	26.12.17		Company arrangements rehearsal of training Games in afternoon	do 6/01
do	27.12.17		Company training. Working party. afternoon - Games	Frosty. 6/01
do Also 36"H.W.1 36.S.W.3 La Basse & Richburg	28.12.17	BWO.146 BOO.147	B" relieved 1/8 L.F. in firing line. B. C. & D. Coy's in front line. A coy in support. Relief commenced at 10 a.m. finished by 11:30 a.m. No casualties. Considerable burial activity.	Frosty. Snow. Ref. Off. 7 & 8
do	29.12.17		In trenches. One patrol. Commencement to reinforce wire Defence Scheme detailed	Frosty. Dull in afternoon. J.S. Off. 9
do	30.12.17	"	" Making concertina coils during day. Wiring continued at night.	Brighter. Too dull for observation. J.S.
do	31.12.17	"	do.	Dull in morning Frosty afternoon J.S.

1.1.18.

A.B.Meakin

Lt Colonel

Cmdg. 1/6 Lan. Fus.

SECRET.

App 1.

COPY No. 11

1/6th Lancashire Fusiliers.

BATTALION OPERATION ORDER No. 141.

In the Field,   3.12.17.

Map Ref. 1:10,000 36c N.W.

1. The 1/6th Lancashire Fusiliers will relieve the 1/8th Lancashire Fusiliers in the line on morning of 4th instant. Relief will commence at 9.0 a.m.

2. Relief will be carried out in the following order:-
   B. Company, 1/6th L.F. moving at 9.0 a.m. to relieve A. Company, 1/8th L.F. in Support.
   A. Company,   " " " " 9.15 a.m. to relieve C. Company, 1/8th L.F. Right Front.
   C. Company,   " " " " 9.30 a.m. to relieve D. Company, 1/8th L.F. Left Front.
   D. Company,   " " " " 9.45 a.m. to relieve B. Company, 1/8th L.F. Centre.

3. Guides:- A. Company will send one Guide from each Keep; B.C. and D. Companies one Guide per Company; all to be at 8th L.F. Headquarters at 8.30 a.m.
   A. Coy, 1/6th L.F. Guides will guide A. Coy 1/8th L.F. to Four Keeps.
   B.   "   "   "   "   "   "   C.   "   "   "   " Marylebone Tr.
   C.   "   "   "   "   "   "   D.   "   "   "   " Harley St.
   D.   "   "   "   "   "   "   B.   "   "   "   " Gunner Siding.

   All Guides to have written instructions saying what Company they are Guides for.
   1/8th L.F. will supply 3 Guides per Company to be at 1/6th L.F. H.Q. at 8. 0 a.m.

4. All trench stores, defence schemes, etc., will be taken over on relief, and lists will be sent to Adjutant by 6.0 p.m. on 4th inst.

5. Relief complete will be wired by word BETH.

6. Water bottles will be filled before moving up. O.C. Coys will see that they have a good supply of anti-trench foot powder.

7. Rations will be delivered to PONT FIXE for C. D. and B. Coys. H.Q. and A. to end of DAWSON STREET. B. Company will do ration carrying for all other Coys. Rations will arrive at usual time- 5.30 p.m.

8. B. Coy loan 1 Lewis Gun to D. Coy.

9. GUM BOOTS will be drawn from Gum Boot Stores, PONT FIXE, (A.14.c.central Nr. GUINCHY Station, in following quantities:-
   A. Company, 40 pairs.
   C.   "   30   "
   D.   "   20   "

10. Outgoing troops will give way to incoming troops.

11. All billets, dugouts, and trenches, will be left in a clean and sanitary condition. O.C. Coys will certify this has been done.

12. ACKNOWLEDGE.

S. Howden   2/Lieut.
a/Adjutant, 1/6th Lan. Fus.

Issued, by Orderly, at 9 a.m. 3.12.17.
Distribution:-
  Copy No. 1. C.O.
   "   "   2. 2/in Command.
   "   "   3. File.
   "   "   4. O.C. A. Coy.
   "   "   5. "   B. "
   "   "   6. "   C. "
   "   "   7. "   D. "
   "   "   8. T.O.
   "   "   9. Q.M.
   "   " 10. Lt. Barker.
   "   " 11. War Diary. ✓
   "   " 12. R.S.M.
   "   " 13. Signals.
   "   " 14. 1/8th L.F.

Van Dran
to Butler

APP. 2

SECRET.   1/6th Lancashire Fusiliers.   COPY No. 6

BATTALION WARNING ORDER No. 142.

Reference Sheet 1:40,000 Bethune.

In the Field, 8.12.17.

The 1/6th Lancashire Fusiliers will be relieved in the line on morning of 10th December, by the 19th Manchester Regiment.

One guide per company and one from H.Q. will meet following advance parties at Drawbridge P.15.d.5.5. at 8.0 a.m. 9th instant. These guides will report to 2/Lieut. King at 7.30 a.m. 9th instant. They must be carefully selected men who know way about trenches.

    1 Officer, H.Q.
    1 Officer per Company.
    1 N.C.O. per Platoon.

The above parties will remain until arrival of their units on 10th instant.

Returned unexchanged dirty socks for clean ones issued will be issued, by orderly, at 8 p.m.

S. Hawdon   2/Lieut.
a/Adjt., 1/6th Lan. Fus.

Distribution:-
Copy No. 1. O.C. A Company.
   " " 2. "   B   "
   " " 3. "   C   "
   " " 4. "   D   "
   " " 5. Sigs. Barker.
   " " 6. 2/Lieut. King.
   " " 7. File.
   " " 8. Spare.

SECRET.   AM 3   COPY No. 10

1/6th Lancashire Fusiliers.
BATTALION OPERATION ORDER No. 143.

Reference Map 1:40,000 BETHUNE.

In the Field, 8.12.17.

1. The 1/6th Lancashire Fusiliers will be relieved in the line by 1/10th Manchester Regiment on the morning of the 10th instant.
2. Advance parties of incoming unit will be met by guides as detailed in warning order No.142.
3. A. Coy 6th L.F. will be relieved by A. Coy 10th Manchesters.
   B. "   "   "   "   "   "   B. "   "   "
   C. "   "   "   "   "   "   C. "   "   "
   D. "   "   "   "   "   "   D. "   "   "
4. GUIDES:- One guide per platoon and one for Battalion H.Q. will report to the I.B.H. at 8.0 a.m. 10th instant; they will each be provided by O.C. Coys, with chit stating what Battalion, Company, and platoon they are to meet. They will proceed under 2/Lieut. W. J. King to Brigade H.Q. F.10.c.9.1. reporting there at 8.30 a.m.
   B. Coy. Guides will know way via Cheyne Walk and Bayswater to Coy H.Q.
   C. "   "   "   "   "   " Cheyne Walk and Orchard Street to Coy H.Q.
   D. "   "   "   "   "   " Cheyne Walk to Coy H.Q.
   A. Coy. Guides will know way via Dawson Street-Queen Street- thence 1 platoon for tunnels via Coldstream Lane.
   1 platoon via Berkshire Street to Company H.Q.
5. All trench stores, defence schemes, list of position calls, L.G. G.E. positions, air photographs and documents relating to this sector will be handed over on relief.   Lists of these will be rendered to Orderly Room not later than 7.0 p.m. 10th instant.
6. Relief complete will be wired by word 'PACK' and in writing, by Orderly, to Battalion H.Q.
7. Gum Boots will be returned to Gum Boot Stores, PONT FIXE, by 8.0 p.m. 9th instant.   O.C. B. Company will arrange to collect these and return to stores.   Receipts will be obtained and sent to Orderly Room.
8. All dug-outs, trenches, latrines, etc., will be left in a clean and sanitary condition.   O.C. Coys will certify this has been done.
9. The 1/6th Lancashire Fusiliers on completion of relief will take over BETHUNE BARRACKS vacated by 4th East Lancashire Regiment.
10. ROUTE:- Canal Bank; left side. (Facing West).
    Distances to be maintained on march as follows:-
    (a.) East of a line BEUVRY-LOCON- 200 yards distance between platoons and groups of 4 vehicles.
    (b.) West of this line 200 yards between Battalions, 100 yards between unit and its Transport.
    (c.) At West of Bridge F.7.a.7.9. leading platoon of each Company will halt; Companies forming up in column of route, and move to the Barracks as a Company, under their Company Commander.
11. Guides, Lieut. Barker and C.S.M.'s, will meet Battalion at Bridge F.7.a.7.9. and guide to quarters.
12. Company Officers' chargers will be at Westminster Bridge at 11.30 a.m. O.C's and Adjutant's chargers at same place at 12.30 p.m.
13. Transport limbers, Mess Cart, etc., will be at Westminster Bridge at 11.0 a.m. 10th instant, for L.G., Signalling, and Orderly Room gear. All periscopes will be sent down on L.G. limbers and handed to I.O. and receipt obtained.
14. One lorry is allotted to remove Q.M. Stores.   Guide will meet it at Transport Lines Road junction F.8.b.7.7. at 7.0 a.m. December 10th. Baggage wagons will also report as above.
15. Arrangements will be made for tea to be issued to Troops on arrival at Barracks.   Dinner at 6.0 p.m.
16. ACKNOWLEDGE.

Issued, by Orderly, at 1145 a.m., 9.12.17.

S Hawden
2/Lieut.
a/Adjt., 1/6th Lan. Fus.

Distribution -overleaf.

Distribution:-

Copy No. 1. O.C.
" 2. 2 in Command.
" 3. File.
" 4. O.C. A. Company.
" 5. "   B.   "
" 6. "   C.   "
" 7. "   D.   "
" 8. Medical Officer.
" 9. Transport Officer and Quartermaster.
" 10. 2/Lieut. E. J. King.
" 11. Lieut. J. S. Barker.
" 12. R. S. M.
" 13. O.C. 1/10th Manchester Regt.
" 14. War Diary.
" 15. Adjutant.
" 16. Spare.

SECRET.   App.4   COPY No. 13.

1/6th Battalion The Lancashire Fusiliers.

CORRECTION TO BATTALION OPERATION ORDER No.143.

PARA.(9.)   Battalion will not go to BETHUNE BARRACKS but to TOBACCO FACTORY, BETHUNE. Map Ref. A.17.b.9.9.

PARA.(11) will read C.Q.M.S's and Sgt. Chadwick (for H.Q.) will report to Lieut. Barker at Battalion H.Q. at 5.0 a.m. 10th instant, and proceed to find new Billets. They will meet Companies at B.7.a.7.9. Bridge, and guide to Billets.

Issued, by Orderly, at 11-25 p.m. 9.12.17.   S. Howden 2/Lieut.
                                                  a/Adjt., 1/6th Lan. Fus.
Distribution:-
Copy No. 1. C.O.
   "   2. 2/in Command.
   "   3. File.
   "   4. O.C. A. Coy.
   "   5.   " B. "
   "   6.   " C. "
   "   7.   " D. "
   "   8. M.O.
   "   9. T.O. and Q.M.
   "   10. 2/Lieut. King.
   "   11. Lieut. Barker.
   "   12. R.S.M.
   "   13. War Diary. ✓
   "   14. Adjutant.
   "   15. Spare.
   "   16. Spare.

SECRET.   COPY No. 14.

1/6th Lancashire Fusiliers.

BATTALION OPERATION ORDER No. 143.   App. 5

Reference Map -1:40.000 BETHUNE.

In the Field, 8.12.17.

1. The 1/6th Lancashire Fusiliers will be relieved in the line by 1/10th Manchester Regiment on the morning of the 10th instant.
2. Advance parties of incoming unit will be met by guides as detailed in Warning Order No.142.
3. A. Coy 6th L.F. will be relieved by A. Coy 10th Manchesters.
   B. "   "   "   "   "   " B. "   "
   C. "   "   "   "   "   " C. "   "
   D. "   "   "   "   "   " D. "   "
4. GUIDES- One guide per platoon and one for Battalion H.Q. will report to the R.S.M. at 6.0 a.m. 10th instant; they will each be provided, by O.C. Coys, with chit stating what Battalion, Company, and platoon, they are to meet. They will proceed under 2/Lieut. R.J. King to Brigade H.Q. M.10.c.9.1. reporting there at 9.30 a.m.
   B. Coy. Guides will know way via Cheyne Walk and Bayswater to Coy H.Q.
   C. "   "   "   "   "   "   Cheyne Walk and Orchard Street to Coy H.Q.
   D. "   "   "   "   "   "   Cheyne Walk to Coy H.Q.
   A. Coy. Guides will know way via Dawson Street-Queen Street- thence
   1 platoon for tunnels via Coldstream Lane.
   1 platoon via Berkshire Street to Company H.Q.
5. All trench stores, defence schemes, list of position calls, L.G. A.A. positions, air photographs and documents relating to this sector will be handed over on relief.   Lists of these will be rendered to Orderly Room not later than 7.0 p.m. 10th instant.
6. Relief complete will be wired by word 'PACK' and in writing, by Orderly, to Battalion H.Q.
7. Gum Boots will be returned to Gum Boot Stores, PONT FIXE, by 5.0 p.m. 9th instant. O.C. D. Company will arrange to collect these and return to Stores.   Receipts will be obtained and sent to Orderly Room.
8. All dug-outs, trenches, latrines, etc., will be left in a clean and sanitary condition.   O.C. Coys will certify this has been done.
9. The 1/6th Lancashire Fusiliers on completion of relief will take over BETHUNE BARRACKS vacated by 4th East Lancashire Regiment.
10. ROUTE- Canal Bank; left side. (Facing West).
    Distances to be maintained on march as follows:-
    (a.) East of a line BEUVRY-LOCON- 200 yards distance between platoons and groups of 4 vehicles.
    (b.) West of this line 500 yards between Battalions, 100 yards between unit and its Transport.
    (c.) At West of Bridge F.7.a.7.9. leading platoon of each Company will halt; Companies forming up in column of route, and move to the Barracks as a Company, under their Company Commander.
11. Guides, Lieut. Barker and C.Q.M.S's, will meet Battalion at Bridge F.7.a.7.9. and guide to quarters.
12. Company Officers' chargers will be at Westminster Bridge at 11.30 a.m. C.O's and Adjutant's chargers at same place at 12.30 p.m.
13. Transport limbers, Mess cart, etc., will be at Westminster Bridge at 11.0 a.m. 10th instant, for L.G., Signalling, and Orderly Room gear. All periscopes will be sent down on L.G. limbers and handed to Q.M. and receipt obtained.
14. One lorry is allotted to remove Q.M. Stores.   Guide will meet it at Transport Lines Road junction F.6.b.7.7. at 7.0 a.m. December 10th. Baggage wagons will also report as above.
15. Arrangements will be made for tea to be issued to Troops on arrival at Barracks.   Dinner at 5.0 p.m.
16. ACKNOWLEDGE.

Issued, by Orderly, at 11-45 a.m., 9.12.17.

S Howden   2/Lieut.
a/Adjt., 1/6th Lan. Fus.

Distribution -overleaf.

Distribution:-   *War Diary*

Copy No. 1. O.C.
" 2. 2/In Command.
" 3. File.
" 4. O.C. A. Company.
" 5. " B. "
" 6. " C. "
" 7. " D. "
" 8. Medical Officer.
" 9. Transport Officer and Quartermaster.
" 10. 2/Lieut. W. J. King.
" 11. Lieut. J. S. Barker.
" 12. R. S. M.
" 13. O.C. 1/10th Manchester Regt.
" 14. War Diary. ✓
" 15. Adjutant.
" 16. Spare.

SECRET.   COPY No. 12

1/6th Bn. Lancashire Fusiliers.
BATTALION OPERATION ORDER NO. 145.

Bethune, 1:40,000   La Bassee } 1:20,000
                    Richebourg}

In the Field, 21.12.17.

1. The 1/6th La. Fus. will relieve 1/5th Man. Regt. in reserve on morning of 22nd instant.   Headquarters at M. 3.b.5.5.

2. The Battalion will march on Birkers at 9.30 a.m. and move off in following order– A. B. H.Q. Band, C. D.
   After leaving main ROUVEY ROAD 20x distance will be maintained between platoons and 100x between transport of equivalent roadspace to a Company.
   Route-   Via LE QUESNOY.

3. DRESS:-   Marching order with packs, steel helmets without covers.

4. Maps, Defence Schemes, photographs, and work policies, and stores, will be taken over and lists sent to Orderly Room by 6.0 p.m., 22nd instant.

5. A. Company will leave 1 Officer, 1 Corporal, and 10 men, as caretakers of Factory until relieved by incoming unit.   Quartermaster will also leave one man for similar purpose.   They will do all necessary cleaning up and obtain certificate stating "Billets handed over in clean condition" before leaving.

6. Lieut. Barker and C.Q.M.S's of each Company, and Sgt. Thompson for Headquarters, will proceed in advance and *lead* companies *to* billets on arrival at GORRE.

7. Transport lines will be taken over from 5th Man. Regt.

8. All stores, blankets &c. will be sent to Quartermaster's Stores by 7.30 a.m.   Officers' kits by 6.0 a.m.
   Blankets must be rolled tightly in bundles of 10; string to tie these up from Quartermaster.

9. Reveille, 5.30 a.m.   Breakfast, 6.15 a.m.   Sick Parade, 7.30 a.m.

10. Officers' chargers to be at Factory at 9.20 a.m.   H.Q. Officers' chargers at H.Q. Mess at same time.

11. Drums will play the Battalion to where the route branches off from main ROUVEY ROAD; they will then return and make their way to 42nd Divisional Wing at VIEHE du ROI.   They will take unexpended portion of day's rations.   Transport Officer will arrange to send their equipment, blankets, and kit, to Divisional Wing.

12. B. Company will detail 1 N.C.O. and 4 men with Lewis Gun complete to report to Headquarters, 1/5th Man. Regt. at 8.0 p.m. this evening. Transport Officer will provide limber to take gun etc.
    This party will leave at 5.40 p.m.

13. Companies will be billetted as follows:- A. B.C. and H.Q. Companies in Chateau.
                                              D. Company in School.

14. ACKNOWLEDGE.

                                          S. Howden 2/Lieut.
                                          a/Adjutant, 1/6th Bn. Fus.

Issued, by Orderly, at 5 p.m.

Distribution -overleaf-.

Distribution:-

Copy No. 1. C. O.
2. 2/in Command.
3. File.
4. C.V.A. Brigade.
5. " " "
6. " " "
7. " " "
8. Medical Officer.
9. Lieut. Barker.
10. Transport Officer.
11. Quartermaster.
12. War Diary.
13. R. S. M.
14. Spare.
15. Adjutant.
16. Spare.

SECRET.   COPY No. 12

1/6th Battalion The Lancashire Fusiliers.

BATTALION MARCHING ORDER No. 146.   App. 4

In the field, 26.12.17.

1. Battalion will move into line on 28th taking over from 8th Lan. Fus. in Left sub Sector.
2. Line will be held as follows:-
   D. Company on Right, taking over from B. Company, 8th Lan. Fus.
   C.   "   Centre,   "   "   " A.   "   "   "   "
   B.   "   on Left,   "   "   " C.   "   "   "   "
   A.   "   Support,   "   "   " D.   "   "   "   "
3. O.C. Companies will arrange to reconnoitre line to-day or 27th instant. On night of 27th/28th one Officer per Company and 1 N.C.O. per platoon will stay in line until Battalion arrives.
   O.C. Companies will arrange all necessary guides for relief and report arrangements to Adjutant.
4. O.C. Companies are reminded to see to-day that their Companies are complete in all details for the line, viz; Iron rations, S.A.A., helmet covers, wire cutters, periscopes, etc.
5. All precautions against trench feet must be commenced at once and particular attention must be paid to this as it is a very wet sector we are about to occupy.
6. Rapid wiring must be practised between now and the move as the wire in front is very bad.
7. GUM BOOTS. O.C. Companies will ascertain if Gum Boots are to be handed over and if they are dry; failing that they will draw from Gum Boot stores.

Issued, by orderly.   S Harden   2/Lieut.
                                                       a/Adjt., 1/6th Lan. Fus.
Distribution- overleaf.

Distribution:-

	Copy No.		
	1.	C.O.	
"	2.	2/in Command.	
"	3.	O.C. A Company.	
"	4.	" B "	
"	5.	" C "	
"	6.	" D "	
"	7.	Transport Officer.	
"	8.	Quartermaster.	
"	9.	Lieut. Barker.	
"	10.	Medical Officer.	
"	11.	R.S.M.	
"	12.	War Diary. ✓	
"	13.	File.	
"	14.	Adjutant.	

SECRET. COPY No. 13

Opp. 8.

1/6th Battalion Lancashire Fusiliers

OPERATION ORDER No. [illegible]

Maps - [illegible] 1/40,000 [illegible] } 1/10,000.

In the Field, 27.IX.17.

1. The 6th Bn. Lancashire Fusiliers will relieve the 5th Battn. Lan. Fus. in the Line (Left Front), on evening of 28th instant.
2. Line will be held as follows:-
   D. Coy. 6th L.F's on Right, taking over from [illegible] Coy. 5th L.F.
   B. " " " Centre, " " " " " "
   A. " " " on Left, " " " " " "
   C. " " " Support, " " " " " "
3. The 5th L.F. will provide 4 guides per Company and 1 for H.Q. Company; these will be at [illegible] Corner at 5.45 p.m. All parties will proceed by [illegible] from Halton Corner.
4. Lieut. Barker, Sgt. Thompson, and Sgt. Chadwick, will proceed in advance and take over stores at Battalion H.Q. They will report to Adjutant, 5th L.F. at 9.0 a.m.
5. Companies will move off at following times:-
   [illegible] Company, [illegible] p.m.
   [illegible] " [illegible] p.m.
   C. " [illegible] p.m.
   [illegible] " [illegible] p.m.
   H.Q. " [illegible] p.m.
   [illegible] yards distance will be maintained between platoons.
6. All Stores, maps, work schemes, etc., will be taken over and lists sent to Orderly Room by [illegible] p.m., 29th instant. Dispositions will be marked on attached map and sent to Orderly Room by [illegible] p.m., 28th instant.
7. Relief complete will be wired by code "[illegible]".
8. 4 dixies per Company (16 in all), will be handed over in exchange. 4 dixies per Company will be taken up to [illegible].
9. Sgt. Smith and 1 Lewis Gunner per Company will proceed with Lewis Guns limbers in advance and have all drums and ammunition etc. ready for Companies to pick up. Companies will have their Lewis Guns ready for loading at 1.30 p.m. at main gate of Chateau.
10. All blankets, packs, and surplus stores, will be stacked on parade ground by 1.30 p.m. Pioneers will take charge of these and load them on returning limbers.
11. Rations will be delivered to Halton Corner each day at 6.30 p.m. and loaded on trolleys; the portion to be cooked will be off-loaded at Cook-house and the remainder delivered to Companies in the line. This will be done by Support Company.
12. All billets will be left clean and sanitary. O.C. Companies will certify this has been done.
13. Reveille, 5.30 a.m. Breakfast, 6.30 a.m. Sick parade, 7.0 a.m.
14. ACKNOWLEDGE.

L.M. Robinson Capt

Adjutant, 1/6th Lan. Fus.

Issued, by Orderly, at 7-0 p.m.

AB3/176

Distribution:-
Copy No. 1. [illegible]
" 2. 2/in Command.
" 3. O.C. A. Company.
" 4. " B. "
" 5. " C. "
" 6. " D. "
" 7. Lieut. Barker.
" 8. Transport Officer.
" 9. Quartermaster.
" 10. Medical Officer.
" 11. R.S.M.
" 12. 5th L.F.
" 13. War Diary.
" 14. File.
" 15. Adjutant.

SECRET.   SCHEME "A".   App. 9.

LEFT BATTALION.   GIVENCHY SECTOR.

Reference Trench Map 1:10,000.

1. **BOUNDARIES.** (1 SOUTH). North end of Berwick South A. 3. a. 9. 6. -
   A. 3. a. 5. 7. - Junction of Willow Road and the Le Plantin-Festubert.
                   (2 NORTH). Junction of RUTLAND ROAD and the front line
   B. 22. a. 3. 1., RUTLAND ROAD (inclusive) to junction with "B" line at
   at B. 21. d. 0. 9. - B. 22. a. 0. - B. 21. c. 2. 4.

2. **DISPOSITION.** 1. Battalion H. Q. B. 26. b. 5. 0. Three Companies
   in the front of "A" line.   One Company in the "B" line.   The
   right and left Companies each have one platoon in "B" line and one
   platoon in the BARTON TRE, and the RICHMOND TRENCH respectively. The
   latter platoons are available for counter-attacks under orders of the
   Company Commanders.
   2. Company H.Q.'s. Right Company BARTON TR., A. 3. a. 6. 9.   Centre
   Company RICHMOND TRENCH, B. 27. b. 3. 4.   Left Company, B. 21. d.4.1.
   Support Company, "B" line B. 26. b. 9. 4.
   One Company of the Support Battalion is at the disposal of the O.C.
   Left Battalion for the purpose of counter-attack.   This Company is
   in "B" line between WILLOW ROAD and SUNKEN RD.

3. **ACTION IN CASE OF ATTACK.**
   (a)   In case of a heavy bombardment of the front line, troops holding
   that line will advance into the open, at least 70 yards in front of
   the line and take up position to repel an attack.
   This action is intended to save the heavy casualties which may occur by
   remaining behind the Breastworks.   The Support Company and the
   Company of the Support Battalion in "B" line, will "Stand to" and send
   an Officer and two runners to report to Battalion H.Q.
   (b)   In case of a raid on any of the posts in the front line, the
   Commanders of the posts on the Right and Left of the post attacked,
   will take their men out into "No mans land" and endeavour to kill
   or capture the raiders when they retire.   The actual post attacked will
   open rapid fire and repel the raiders.
   (c)   In case of an attack developing and any part of "A" line is
   broken, Company Commanders of the Right and Left companies will counter-
   attack with their support platoons.   The Officer Commanding the
   Support Company and the Company of the Support Battalion will ensure
   that all their Officers and N.C.Os know the shortest way, both over the
   top and up the Communication Trenches, from their posts to the Front
   Line, in case they are required to counter-attack.

4. **S.O.S.** The S.O.S. consists of GREEN ROCKETS sent up in pairs, the
   signal to be continued until the Artillery open fire, and must be
   confirmed immediately by written message.
   A Company or Battalion receiving an S.O.S signal from the troops of a
   Unit on its flank *will not pass it on to the next unit on the flank*
   unless the S.O.S. is repeated on its own front also.
   The Artillery must be informed immediately its fire is no longer required.

5. **RETALIATION FIRE.** If any portion of his front is shelled, the
   Company Commander will inform B.H.Q. by the code word "TRALYTE", then
   giving the number of rounds which the enemy has fired and the approximate
   direction of the guns firing.   In the case of Trench Mortars being
   used the code word "GRANITE HEAVY" followed as above by the number
   of rounds and the approximate direction.   Retaliation will not be
   asked for if only a few rounds are fired.

6. This scheme will be handed over on relief.

Issued, by orderly, at ____ a.m.   F.K. Robinson
                        29.12.17   Adjt., 1/5th Lon. Fus.   Captain,

Distribution:-
   A. Company.
   B.   "
   C.   "
   D.   "
   Company of Support Batta.
   3 File copies.

CONFIDENTIAL.

WAR DIARY

of

1/6th Battalion The Lancashire Fusiliers

From 1.1.18   To 31.1.18.

Volume No 30.

APP. 1, 2, 3, 4, 5, 6, 7, 8, 9, 10

WAR DIARY
or
INTELLIGENCE SUMMARY.

(Erase heading not required.)

Army Form C. 2118.

VOL. 30

1/6 LANCASHIRE FUSILIERS.

Place	Hour, Date, Place Date	Orders.	Summary of Events and Information	Remarks and references to Appendices Weather.	App. No.	Signature
LA BASSÉE 36ᵉ N.W. RICHEBOURG 36 S.W. (S 26 b 50)	1.1.18	B.W.O. 148.	In the trenches. Patrols and wiring. Usual trench routine. Bn. Warning Order issued	Frosty but dull.	1	23/1/18 J.S.
"	2.1.18		" "	Still dull but not so frosty.		488 J.S.
"	3.1.18.	B.O.O. 149.	Batt'n. relieved in the morning by 1/8 Lanc. Fus. and were disposed thus. B.H.Q. at WINDY CORNER A & B Coy in KEEPS A 9 c. "C" coy in Support Billets A 8 c 64, D coy in support to 1/8 Lanc Fus. in area 2 A b d. Ref. LA BASSÉE 1:10,000 A 8 c 82.	Very clear & frosty.	2	25 514 J.S.
LA BASSÉE 36ᵉ N.W. A 8 c 82.	4.1.18		Day & night working parties supplied by A. B & C. coys.	Dulls. Frost continuing		25 514 J.S.
"	5.1.18.		Working parties drawn from all Coys. Party three coys at baths	Still frosty		25 513 J.S.
"	6.1.18.		Small party at baths. Working parties continued. Working on repair'g keeps	Very dull. Milder at night		25 510 J.S.
"	7.1.18.		Coys. still employed by R.E's. Defence scheme detailed	Fresh & dully. Frost at night	3	25 510 J.S.
"	8.1.18.		Working parties eased to be found after midnight 8/9ᵗʰ Repairing keeps.	Frosty. Raining		25 524 J.S.
LA BASSÉE 36ᵉ N.W. RICHEBOURG 36 S.W. (S 26 b 50)	9.1.18.		Bn. relieved 1/8 L.F. in firing line A 3 b 99 to S 32 c 35/5 A.B & C Coys in Front Line, "D" Coy in Support. Relief commenced about 10 a.m. Completed midday No casualties. 1 E.A. over after relief partially completed	Still Raining. Raining all afternoon.	4	25 525 J.S.
"	10.1.18		Cleaning trenches. Making "gooseberries" & "Concertinas". Wiring at night.	Fresh. Fairly clear.	5	25 531 J.S.
"	11.1.18.		Ordinary trench routine. Wiring by night.	Fresh but dull		27 528 J.S.

WAR DIARY or INTELLIGENCE SUMMARY.

Army Form C. 2118.

VOL 30

1/6 LANCASHIRE FUSILIERS

Place	Hour, Date, Date	Orders	Summary of Events and Information	Remarks and references to Appendices. Weather	App. No.	Strength	Signature
LA BASSÉE 36c N.W. RICHEBOURG 36 S.W. (S 26 & 50)	12/1/18		Cleaning trenches. Making연ceatina wire. Wiring by night.	Dull but milder		28 524	JS
"	13/1/18	B.OO. 151.	Ordinary trench routine. Still wiring for new defended localities.	Clear & sharp?	6.	27 522	JS
"	14/1/18	B.O.O. 151. Corrigendum	"	Dull. Snowing.	7	28 589	JS
"	15/1/18		Very busy wiring ESLAND Post 4/8.4. Usual routine by day.	Fresh, Bright		26 526	JS
"	16/1/18		Repairing trenches. Falls caused by heavy rain a/c front. Ordinary routine.	Dull Heavy rain		26 505	JS
BEUVRY 36 B13 N.E. 2. 1/10,000 E 6 C	17/1/18	B.O.O. 151. Attendum/Add.	Battalion relieved at midday by 1/10 Manchester Regiment & then marched to FERME du ROI near BETHUNE. Ref. BEUVRY MAP 1:10,000 E.6.c. No casualties during relief. Last arrivals about 5 p.m.	Very heavy rain all day.	8.	26 477	JS
"	18/1/18		A, B & D Coy's on working parties in GORE or LOISNE AREAS. 'C' Coy bathing, refitting & cleaning up.	Frost about Bad underfoot.		26 480	JS
"	19/1/18		A, C & D Coy. working parties. a.m 18th inst. 'B' Coy at baths, changing clothing, refitting equipment.	Weather much improved. Roads drying	9	29 484	JS
"	20/1/18		B, C & D Coy. working parties "A" by cleaning up etc.	Quite mild		29 492	JS
"	21/1/18		A, B & C " " 'D' refitting. No baths	Fresh & bright		28 563	JS
"	22/1/18		A, C & D " " All available men working on new stables	Very mild		29 425	JS
"	23/1/18		B & C by part 60 men & 1 off. to CAMBRIN attached to Australian Tunnelling Coy. Other Coys on working parties as before. Officer visit R.F.C. at HESDIGNEUL	Duller & colder.		29 503	JS

WAR DIARY
or
INTELLIGENCE SUMMARY.
(Erase heading not required.)

Army Form C. 2118.

Vol. 30
1/6 LANCASHIRE FUSILIERS.

Place	Date	Hour, Place Orders	Summary of Events and Information	Remarks and references to Appendices	Weather		
BEUVRY. 38.B. N.E.2 15.000. E.6.C.	24/1/18		A. B & D coys still supplying men for same working parties		Very Bright	Sugt Off to Lystn	J.S.
	25/1/18		Ditto		Mild		J.S
	26/1/18		'C' Coy men returned in afternoon from CAMBRIN. A B & D on same duty	Bright		95 503	J.S
	27/1/18		Working parties cancelled. Church Parade at 11.30 a.m. Shores Reliurant in afternoon		Mild	27 516	J.S
	28/1/18		A.B & C. coys sent by motor transport to work in CAMBRIN AREA. D Coy provided 37 men on detailed duty. two officers sent home for 6 months		Hazy in morning cleared later.	27 511	J.S
Ditto F.10.c.	29/1/18.	B.O.O. 152	B's relieved 1/7 Manchester Regt. in Bde. Reserve of right Bde of Div.n Sector at LE PREOL. Relief complete by 12 noon. Companies on Coy return all day about 4 p.m.		A slight haze	96 506	J.S
	30/1/18		A B & C Corps working on trench repairs under the 428 Fld Coy R.E. D Coy Puvish working partie		Sunny Visibility Poor.	25.47/5 23-465	10. J.S W.S
	31/1/18		ditto		Ditto	23-466	W.S

SECRET.   1/6th Battalion The Lancashire Fusiliers.   COPY No. 7
         BATTALION ORDERS No. 148.   App. 1.
                                          In the Field, 1.1.16.

Reference Maps BETHUNE 1:40,000,
                RICHEBOURG } 1:10,000.
                LA BASSEE

1. 8th Lan. Fus. will relieve 6th Lan. Fus. on 3rd January, commencing
    about 10.0 a.m.
2. On relief Companies will move as follows:-
    A. Company,   to Garrison of Keeps.
    B.   "   " Support Billets.
    C.   "   "   "   "
    D.   "   " support of 8th Lan. Fus. in trench now occupied by
    C. Company, 7th Lan. Fus.
3. An Officer of A. Company and C.Q.M.S's of B. and C. Companies
    report to Adjutant at 9.0 a.m. to-morrow, to proceed to 7th Lan. Fus.
    H.Q. and arrange accommodation of these Companies.
4. ACKNOWLEDGE.
                                          h M Robinson
Issued, by Orderly, at ____ p.m.   Captain,
         Distribution:-   Ajt., 1/6th Lan. Fus.
    Copy No. 1. O.C. A. Company.
      "   " 2. "   B.   "
      "   " 3. "   C.   "
      "   " 4. "   D.   "
      "   " 5. Quartermaster.
      "   " 6. Transport Officer.
      "   " 7. War Diary.
      "   " 8. File.

SECRET.   App. 2.   COPY No. 9

1/6th Battalion The Lancashire Fusiliers.
BATTALION OPERATION ORDERS No. 149.
                                                                               In the Field, 2.1.18.

Reference Maps BETHUNE 1:40.000
                 RICHEBOURG } 1:10.000
                 LA BASSEE }

1. 8th Lan. Fus. will relieve 6th Lan. Fus. on January 3rd, commencing with D. Company, 6th L.F. about 11.0 a.m.
2. Companies will be relieved in following order:-

8th L.F. will relieve	6th L.F.	on relief Coys move to:-
B. Coy.	D. Coy.	Support of 8th L.F.
A. "	C. "	Support billets.
D. "	B. "	Support billets.
C. "	A. "	Garrison of Keeps.

     O.C. D. Company will reconnoitre accommodation for his Company on morning of 3rd January. Accommodation for A. B. and C. Companies already reconnoitred.

3. No guides required.
4. (a) A N.C.O. of each Company of 8th L.F. will report at 9.0 a.m. to Company Commanders concerned to take over stores.
    (b) All Intelligence maps, defence schemes, log books, work policies, etc., to be handed over.
    (c) Certificates of cleanliness of trenches must be obtained from incoming Companies.
    (d) Receipts for all documents and stores handed over to be sent to Orderly Room by 6.0 p.m., 4th January.
5. Completion of relief will be reported by O.C. Coy on the way down. O.C. D. Coy will send a runner.
6. Detail of working parties while Battalion is in Support will be issued later.
7. Lieut. J. S. Barker will proceed in advance to take over new H.Q.
8. ACKNOWLEDGE.

                                                W. Robinson.   Captain,
Issued, by Orderly, at 7.0 p.m.   Adjt., 1/6th Lan. Fus.

Distribution:-

Copy No. 1.   O.C. A. Company.
"   "   2.   "   B.   "
"   "   3.   "   C.   "
"   "   4.   "   D.   "
"   "   5.   Quartermaster.
"   "   6.   Lieut. J. S. Barker.
"   "   7.   Transport Officer.
"   "   8.   Medical Officer.
"   "   9.   War Diary.
"   " 10.   File.
"   " 11.   Spare.
"   " 12.   Spare.

SECRET.   DEFENCE SCHEME, SUPPORT BATTALION.   App.3.   COPY No. 6

Reference Maps:-
Trench Map,   1:10,000
LA BASSEE   GIVENCHY, Secret,
RICHEBOURG.   Map No.10.

1.   The Battalion is in support of the Left Brigade of Divisional Sector.

2.   (a) **Front Line.** Two Battalions in the Front Line of Brigade Sector.

        (b) **Support Battalion.** Battalion H.Q. A.14.a.9.9.
                                     Two Coys. in GIVENCHY KEEP.
                                                   MAIRIE REDOUBT.
                                                   M. LEWIS ROAD WEST.
                                                   MOAT FARM.
                                                   HERTS REDOUBT.

             With Company H.Q. in Herts Redoubt.

             One Company at WINDY CORNER, with Company H.Q. at A.2.d.8.4.

             One Company in 'B. Line' in support of Left Battalion with Company H.Q. at A.2.b.4.8.

3.   PRINCIPLES OF DEFENCE. (a) The two Companies garrisoning the Keeps will hold out at all costs. Should the enemy succeed in penetrating the Front Line the Keeps will serve to break their advance until a counter-attack drives them back.

        (b) The Company at WINDY CORNER will be prepared on receipt of orders to
            (1) Occupy the line GUNNER SIDING- WOOD LANE- CALEDONIAN ROAD- WITCH GUT.
            (2) Counter-attack across the open.
            (3) Form a Defence Flank N. and S. of GIVENCHY RIDGE.

        (c) The Company in support of the Left Battalion is intended primarily as a garrison of the O.B. Line. It may be used to counter-attack if required by the O.C. Left Battalion.

             The O.C. the Companies at WINDY CORNER and in support of the Left Battalion will make themselves acquainted with all routes leading to the Front Line, that they would use if required to make a counter-attack.

4.   S.O.S. SIGNAL. - Consists of Red Rockets sent up in pairs. It will be sent up by Front Line Companies, repeated by Battalion H.Q., and continued until the Artillery open fire.

5.   AMMUNITION DUMPS. - are situated at all Company H.Q. and in Keeps. They can be replenished from Battalion H.Q. as required.

        RATIONS. There is a Reserve Ration Dump in each Keep.

                                                    L.Robinson
                                                         Captain,
                                                    Adjutant, 1/6th Lan. Fus.

ACKNOWLEDGE.

Issued, by Orderly. at 6.0 a.m.
                       V.I.M.
Distribution:-
    Copy No. 1.   O.C. A. Company.
        "   2.   "   B.   "
        "   3.   "   C.   "
        "   4.   "   D.   "
        "   5.   File.
        "   6.   War Diary. ✓
        "   7.   File. Spare.

Secret 2/Lt Sutherland

SECRET.   COPY No. 8

1/6th Battalion The Lancashire Fusiliers.

BATTALION OPERATION ORDER No. 150.

Reference Maps:- BETHUNE, 1:40,000   RICHEBOURG) 1:10,000
                                     LA BASSEE,)

In the field, 8. 1. 18.

1. 6th Lan. Fus. will relieve 8th Lan. Fus. on Left Front Brigade Sector on 9th January.
2. Companies will move up in the following order:- (Head of A. Coy will leave HERTS AVENUE at 9.0 a.m.)
   A. Company.   Right Company in Line.)
   B.   "   Left Company in Line.)
   C.   "   Centre.   )
   D.   "   Support.   )
   Battn. H.Q.   ) 200x between platoons.
   If visibility is good 200x between sections will be maintained. D. Coy will not move until C. Coy is clear of BARNTON ROAD.
3. Route for A. and B. Companies will be via HERTS AVENUE - A.B. and C. Companies via LE PLANTIN- BARNTON ROAD, D. Company via 'B' Line.
4. 2/Lieut. J. Sutherland will proceed to 6th Lan. Fus. H.Q. on the afternoon of the 8th January, to arrange details of taking over Stores, Intelligence etc.
   O. C. Coys will send a N.C.O. representative to the H.Q. of the Company to be taken over from by 9.0 a.m. on the 9th January to check Stores to be taken over and obtain any information re changes in the Company Front.
5. All Stores, Maps, Defence Schemes, Work policies, etc., will be handed over. Companies will leave a N.C.O. behind for this purpose. Lieut. J. S. Barker will remain at Battalion H.Q. to hand over to incoming Unit.
   Certificates of cleanliness will be obtained. All receipts and Certificates will be sent to Orderly Room by 6.0 p.m., 9th instant.
6. Working parties will cease to be found after mid-night, 8th and 9th instant.
7. Ration and water arrangements will be the same as during the last tour
8. ACKNOWLEDGE.

                                                    R. Robinson
Issued, by orderly, at 12-Noon a.m.
                                                    Captain,
                                                    Adjt., 1/6th Lan. Fus.

Distribution:-
  Copy No. 1. O.C. A. Company.
   "   " 2.   "   B.   "
   "   " 3.   "   C.   "
   "   " 4.   "   D.   "
   "   " 5. Quartermaster and
                  Transport Officer.
   "   " 6. 2/Lieut. J. Sutherland.
   "   " 7. Lieut. J. S. Barker.
   "   " 8. War Diary.
   "   " 9. File.
   "   " 10. 8th Lan. Fus.
   "   " 11. Spare.

LB.

SECRET.   COPY No. 6

DEFENCE SCHEME.
App. 5

ANY BATTALION.

Reference Map, LA BASSEE)
                MORBECQUE) 1:10,000.

1. The Battalion holds the Left Brigade Left Sector.

2. BOUNDARIES. (a.) South. North end of WARWICK NORTH (A. 3.c.35.20.)
   – A. 3.c.65.75. – Junction of WILLOW ROAD and the ST. ELUNIE-WARWICK
   ROAD (A. 3.c.40.40.)
   (b.) North Junction of SHETLAND ROAD and front line (S. 22.c.38.15.)
   SHETLAND ROAD (inclusive) to its junction with B.... line at S. 21.a.9.)
   – A. 23.c.50.50. – A. 15.c.00.00.

3. DISPOSITIONS. –
   Three Companies in front line, two in support in 'B' Line, (1 Company by
   Support Battalion).
   Battalion Headquarters –   S. 26.b.50.
   RIGHT Company A.C. in BARNTON TRENCH, A. 3.a.58 with Company HQ Reserve
   in front line in BARNTON NORTH CENTRE and SOUTH, and platoon in BARNTON
   fell in support.
   Centre Company B.C. in RICHMOND TERRACE S. 27.b.30. with 1 platoon in
   front line in DOVER TRENCH, and 1 platoon in support in RICHMOND
   TRENCH.
   Left Company C.C. in RICHMOND TERRACE S. 27.b.39. with 3 sections in
   front line in DOVER TRENCH by day and 5 sections by night. 1 L.G.
   section at junction of RICHMOND TRENCH and SHETLAND ROAD, and 2
   sections in support in RICHMOND TRENCH by day, and 1 section by night.
   Right Support Company D.C. in 'B' Line at A. 2.a.44. with Company in 'B'
   Line.
   Left Support Company E.C. in 'B' Line at S. 26.b.67. with Company in
   'B' Line.

4. ACTION IN CASE OF ATTACK.
   (a.) All posts in front line will hold out at all costs. There will
   be no withdrawal.
   (b.) In the event of any of the front line posts being raided the
   Commanders of the Posts on both flanks will take their men into
   'no mans land' and kill or capture the raiders as they retire. The
   posts attacked will open rapid fire and repel the raiders.
   (c.) In case of an attack developing on a large scale, Commanders of
   Companies in the line will use their reserves to counter-attack if
   the enemy penetrates into the front system. The Commanders of
   both Support Companies will send 2 runners to Battalion H... and
   "stand to". As these Companies may be required to counter-
   attack all Officers should make themselves acquainted with all
   routes up to the line.

5. DEFENCE OF DEFENCE SYSTEM.
   (a.) Each Company area is being arranged for all-round defence.
   The gap between the Centre and Right Company is being NICKERN wired
   right across and will form a pocket with apex on 'B' line should
   the enemy penetrate it. The whole of this ground is capable of
   being swept by L.G. and rifle fire from both flanks.
   (b.) The Left Support Company will be prepared to occupy a Post in
   SHETLAND ROAD at S. 21.a.75. only in the event of the Brigade on the
   left being driven back, and if ordered to do so to man SHETLAND
   ROAD with the whole Company.

6. S.O.S. The S.O.S. consists of Golden Rain Rockets, continued until
   the Artillery open fire. This must be confirmed immediately by a written
   message. A Company receiving the S.O.S. from a Unit on the flank will
   not pass it on. Battalion H... must be informed immediately the fire
   is no longer required.

7. RETALIATION SCHEME. If any portion of this front is shelled the Company
   Commander will inform Battalion H... by the code word "TRIXIE", then
   giving the number of rounds which the enemy has fired and the approximate
   direction of the guns firing. In the case of Trench Mortars being used
   the code word "FRANTIC BILL" followed as above by the number of rounds
   and the approximate direction. Retaliation will not be asked for if
   only a few rounds are fired.

                                                                   P.T.O.

c. HAND OVER.
d. ACKNOWLEDGE.

LtRobinson

Issued by orderly at 11.0 am 11/1/18   Adjutant, 1/5th Bn. Fus.   Captain,
AB 3/481

Distribution:-

Copy No. 1.   O.C. A Company.
"   "   2.   "   " B.   "
"   "   3.   "   " C.   "
"   "   4.   "   " D.   "
"   "   5.   Company of Support Battalion.
"   "   6.   War Diary.
"   "   7.   File.
"   "   8.   File.

SECRET.   COPY No. 10

1/6th Battalion The Lancashire Fusiliers.
BATTALION OPERATION ORDER No. 151.

App. 6

Reference-   BETHUNE Combined Sheet,   1:40,000.

1. 1/10th Manchester Regiment will relieve 1/6th Lancashire Fusiliers in Brigade Left Sector on 15th January.   On relief 6th Lan. Fus. will go into Divisional Reserve at FERME du ROI, E. 6. c.
2. Companies will be relieved in the following order:-
   A. Coy. 6th L.F. by D. Coy. 1/10th Manchester Regt.
   C. "   "   "   " B. "   "   "   "
   B. "   "   "   " A. "   "   "   "
   D. "   "   "   " C. "   "   "   "

   On relief Companies will march to FERME du ROI via ESTUBERT X Roads TUNING FORK N. LE JUENIN.
3. Distance of 200 yards will be maintained between platoons and groups of 4 vehicles East of BEUVRY LOCON Line.   West of this Line a distance of 100 yards between transport and the Battalion.
4. O.C. Companies will detail 1 guide per Company H.Q. and 1 for each platoon to be at Battalion H.Q. by 10.0 a.m., on 15th January; they will report to Adjutant, and proceed under 2/Lieut. Sutherland to ESTAMINET CORNER by 11.30 a.m.
5. All trench stores, L.G. M.G. positions, maps, defence schemes, schemes of work and wiring in progress, and documents relating to the Sector will be handed over.   Receipted lists of trench stores will be forwarded to Orderly Room by 6.0 p.m., 15th January.
6. Completion of relief will be reported to Battalion H.Q. by O.C. Companies on the way down.   O.C. A. Company will send a runner.
7. ACKNOWLEDGE.

ADMINISTRATIVE INSTRUCTIONS.

1. Refilling point-   No change.
2. Supply wagons will deliver rations for consumption 16th January in new area.
3. Baggage wagons will report to Transport Lines on evening of 14th January.   One motor lorry is allotted to the Battalion or equivalent horse transport for one trip.   This lorry will be taken over from the 1/10th Manchester Regt.
4. Mess Cart, Maltese Cart, and Company L.G. limbers will be at ESTAMINET CORNER by noon 15th January.
4. Billeting party consisting of the 4 C.Q.M.S's under the Quartermaster will proceed to FERME du ROI on morning of the 14th January and arrange accomodation etc.

Issued, by Orderly, at 5:30 p.m., 13.1.18.

L Robinson
Captain,
Adjutant, 1/6th Lan. Fus.

Distribution:-

   Copy No. 1.   O.C. A. Company.
    "   "   2.   "   B.   "
    "   "   3.   "   C.   "
    "   "   4.   "   D.   "
    "   "   5.   Quartermaster.
    "   "   6.   Transport Officer.
    "   "   7.   Signals Officer.
    "   "   8.   Intelligence Officer.
    "   "   9.   Medical Officer.
    "   " 10.   War Diary.
    "   " 11.   File.
    "   " 12.   File.

App. 7.

SECRET.   COPY No. 8

CORRIGENDUM TO BATTALION OPERATION ORDER No. 151.

1. The relief of 6th Lan. Fus. by 1,10th Manchester Regt. has been postponed until further orders.
2. ACKNOWLEDGE.

Issued, by Orderly, at 11.30 a.m., 14.1.18.

L.M.Robinson
Captain,
Adjutant, 1/6th Lan. Fus.

Distribution:-
Copy No. 1. O.C. A. Coy.
"   2. " B. "
"   3. " C. "
"   4. " D. "
"   5. Quartermaster.   P.T.O.

```
Copy No.  6.   Transport Officer.
  "       7.   Signals Officer.
  "       8.   Intelligence Officer. ✓
  "       9.   War Diary.
  "      10.   File.
  "      11.   1/10th Man. Regt.
  "      12.   Medical Officer.
```

SECRET.   App.8   COPY No. 9

1/6th Battalion The Lancashire Fusiliers.

ADDENDUM No. 1. to BATTALION OPERATION ORDER No. 151.

1. The Relief detailed in Battalion Operation Order No. 151. will take place on the 17th January.

   All dates in above order will be amended by adding on 2 days.

2. ACKNOWLEDGE.

Issued, by Orderly, at 11.55 a.m., 16.1.18.

AB3/584.

J Sutherland

Captain,
Adjutant, 1/6th Lan. Fus.

Distribution:-

Copy No. 1. O.C. A. Company.
"   2. "   B.   "
"   3. "   C.   "
"   4. "   D.   "
"   5. Quartermaster.
"   6. Transport Officer.
"   7. Signals.
"   8. Intelligence Officer.
"   9. War Diary.
"   10. Medical Officer.
"   11. 1/10th Manch. Regt.
"   12. File.

SECRET.   O.C. A. Company,
          "   B. "
          "   C. "
          "   D. "   File.

                War Diary.

Reference BETHUNE Combined Sheet 1:40,000.

    The Reserve Brigade has certain tasks allotted
to it in case of attack, which are as follows:-
(1.) IN CASE OF ATTACK ON DIVISIONAL FRONT.
    (a) To move at 1½ hours notice.
    (b) To occupy Village Line, with the object of
        either counter-attacking from it or holding
        it as a defensive position.
    (c) To occupy the switch line.
(2.) IN CASE OF ATTACK OF DIVISION ON RIGHT.
    (a) To occupy a defensive flank on Line FOSSE 9-
        CAMBRIN.
    (b) To reinforce left Brigade of Division on
        Right.   This ground has been reconnoitred
        to-day.
(3.) IN CASE OF ATTACK ON DIVISION ON LEFT.
    (a) To prolong the Defensive Flank found by the
        Brigades in the GIVENCHY SECTOR and occupy
        the Line EPINETTE X- LE TOURET Central
        MESPLAUX Group (Northern Work X 86.)
        This ground will be reconnoitred to-morrow.

                        L. Robinson
                                  Captain,
                        Adjt., 1/6th Lan. Fus.

SECRET.   COPY No. 11

1/6th Battalion The Lancashire Fusiliers

BATTALION OPERATION ORDER No. 152.

Reference Maps Combined Sheet, 1:40,000 BETHUNE,
LA BASSEE Sheet, 1:10,000

In the Field,   27.1.18.

1. 6th Lan. Fus. will relieve 7th Manchester Regt. in Brigade Reserve of right Brigade of Divisional Sector on 29th January, at LE PREOL.

2. All trench stores, L.G. A.A. positions, documents relating to the Sector will be taken over, and receipted lists sent to Orderly Room by 6.0 p.m., 29th January.

3. The Quartermaster, all C.Q.M.S's, and 1 N.C.O. for Battalion H.Q. (to be detailed by Signals Officer) will proceed to LE PREOL, leaving here at 9.0 a.m. to-morrow to arrange accomodation and billets. The party will return when they have completed arrangements and act as guides on 29th January.

4. Details of Working parties to be found during the time the Battalion is in Brigade Reserve will be issued separately.

5. A. B. and C. Companies will furnish Working Parties on 29th January: they will march back direct from there to LE PREOL.

6. Details of march as follows:-
   D. Company leave PRIME du BOIS .... 9. 0 a.m.
   Company H.Q. and details of A.)
   B. and C. Companies.   ) ... ... 9.15 a.m.
   Battalion H.Q.   9.30 a.m.
   ROUTE:- Southern Canal Bank Road leading from P.9.b.86 to LE PREOL.
   Battalion H.Q. to be clear of Draw Bridge at P.3.c. by 10.15 a.m.

7. Relief complete will be wired to Battalion H.Q. by Code-word 'INSERT'.

8. ACKNOWLEDGE.

ADMINISTRATIVE INSTRUCTIONS.

1. Baggage wagons, and 1 motor lorry if available, report to Transport Lines at 7.0 a.m. on 29th January. If present restrictions are still in force supply wagons will report with transport wagons. Wagons must not move empty.

2. Supplies will be drawn by 1st Line Transport.

3. Transport Lines of 7th Manchester Regt. will be taken over.

4. Mobile reserve will be exchanged.

5. Blankets and all stores and baggage to be moved will be stacked at Quartermaster's Stores by 7.30 a.m., 29th January. Officers baggage will be stacked at Chateau at 7.30 a.m. also.

Issued, by orderly, at 6.45 p.m., 27.1.18.   L.A.Robinson.
                                                      Captain,
                                                Adjutant, 1/6th Lan. Fus.

Distribution:-
   Copy No. 1. O.C. A. Company.
      "   2. "   B.   "
      "   3. "   C.   "
      "   4. "   D.   "
      "   5. Quartermaster.
      "   6. Transport Officer.
      "   7. Medical Officer.
      "   8. 7th Manchester Regt.
      "   9. 2/Lieut. Truesdale.
      "   10. R. S. M.
      "   11. War Diary. ✓
      "   12. Spare.
      "   13. Spare.
      "   14. File.

LB.

2/Lt Sutherland.

www.ingramcontent.com/pod-product-compliance
Lightning Source LLC
Chambersburg PA
CBHW081554160426
43191CB00011B/1930